AF615125

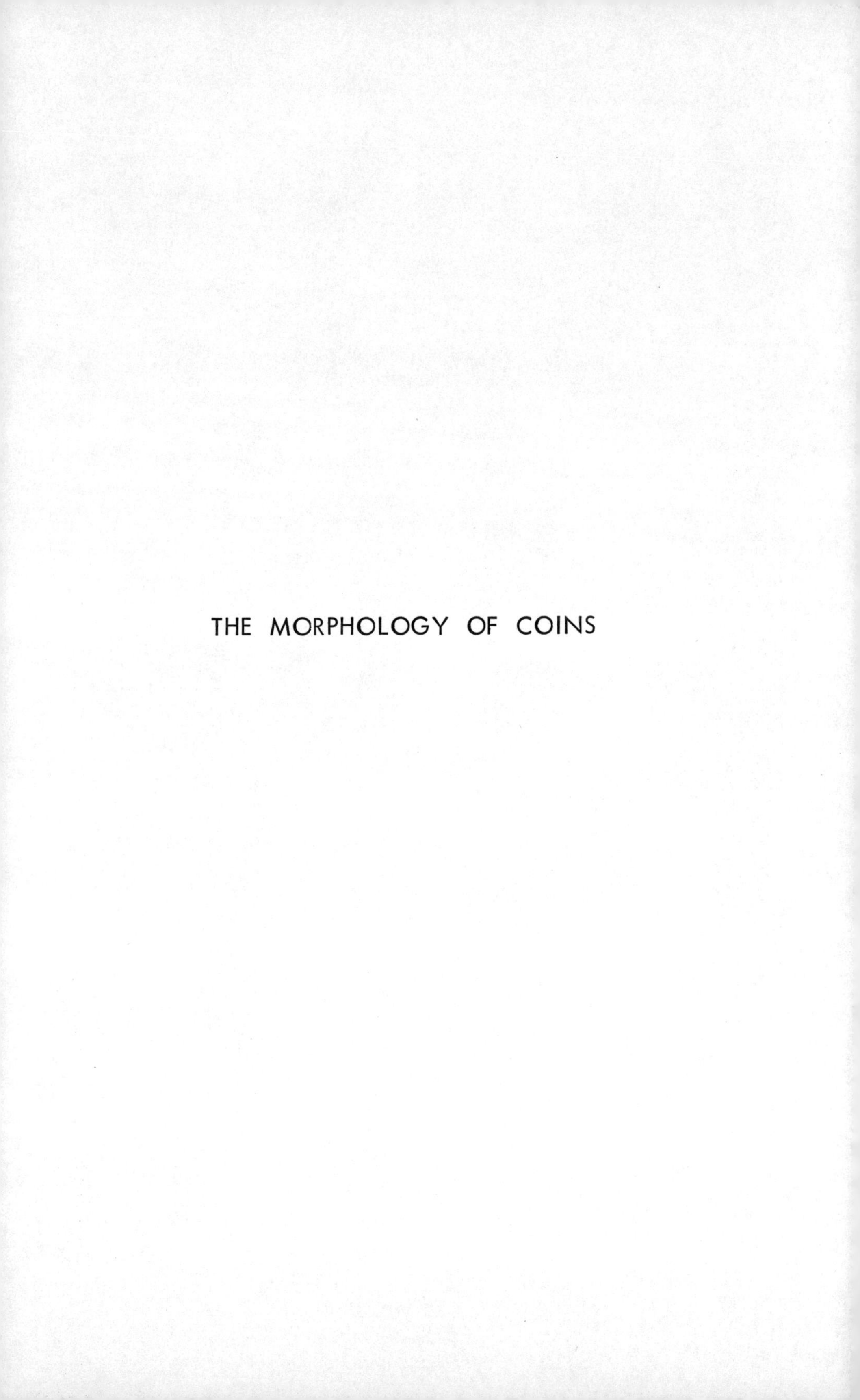

THE MORPHOLOGY OF COINS

THE MORPHOLOGY OF COINS.

BY

C. F. KEARY, M.A., F.S.A.

ARGONAUT, INC., PUBLISHERS
CHICAGO MCMLXX

KEARY, C.F. **THE MORPHOLOGY OF COINS.** *SBN 8244-0082-8. 96 pp. + 6 pl. Rp. 1885/1886* *$ 10.00*

An indispensable general view of the history and evolution of the gradual changes in form and style of ancient and mediaeval coin-types. For the student of art and numismatics.

ARGONAUT INC., PUBLISHERS
737 North Michigan Avenue
Chicago, Illinois 60611

THE MORPHOLOGY OF COINS.

I.—The Greek Family.

By the morphology of coins I mean the history of those changes in their form which have resulted, not from definite historical events, but from influences which are always present, and are always affecting in a greater or less degree the evolution of coins. These influences in their turn are the result of forces common to human nature, and in many respects analogous to those which have produced the variations in form in the animal and vegetable kingdoms. It is to Mr. Evans that we owe the inauguration of this form of inquiry, for his studies of the *Coins of the Ancient Britons* afford, I will not say merely the most important, but the sole example of an inquiry in this direction. Since writing his larger work on the coins of the Ancient Britons, Mr. Evans has further emphasized this particular aspect of his researches in a lecture delivered before the Royal Institution, and called the *Coinage of the Ancient Britons and Natural Selection*, in which he has pointed out many ways in which the development of coin-types bears analogy to the natural laws for the evolution of species. Of recent years, again, General Pitt-Rivers, taking up the same kind of morphological study in relation to other objects, has arranged a collection of different kinds of human implements, and has communicated several highly interesting papers upon their morphology, of which his monograph upon *Locks and Keys* is perhaps the most complete. Following the steps of these distinguished anthropologists, I have endeavoured to give such a classification of coins as may illustrate the development "from the homogeneous to the heterogeneous" of this important instrument in human civilisation.

Mr. Evans's essay on the *Coinage of the Ancient Britons and Natural Selection* was concerned more with the influences which determined the engravers in the choice and arrangement of their types, than with the influences which had determined the form of the coinage as a whole. This method of treatment, which considers coin-types in the light of designs, and their evolution as a phase in the history of the art of design, would find ample scope for its researches in the department of numismatics. But it is not with that aspect of the subject that I propose to deal in the present article. In the present essay I propose to consider the development of coins only in so far as it is a functional development, that is to say, brought about by the special function which coins are designed to fulfil. Certain particular classes, or let me say *species* of coins have come to be so much more than mere media of exchange, that we are apt—numismatists are especially apt—to forget that to be a medium of exchange is all that a coin is required by its nature to be. The Greek and Roman coinages, and some few special coinages descended from the Greek and Roman, have happened to acquire so many features of artistic excellence or archæological value, and as such have attracted such a large or exclusive amount of attention, that numismatists are inclined to think that all coins must necessarily have some of the qualities which we admire in these selected species. Those who have been concerned chiefly with coins rich in archæological interest have been disposed to look in all classes of coins for much more than they could reasonably find there. They have discovered maps, plans, brief chronicles, monuments, in many cases where, had they looked a little closer, and examined the issues immediately preceding and following the one with which they were actually dealing, they would have seen that the coin-type of the latter was determined by circumstances far antecedent to the simple desires of the striker of the coins. In former times people taking up coin-types in the way I have described made the most ridiculous guesses at their meaning. It has not been uncommon for them to read in some simple arrangement of lines the map or plan of a city or a fortification. Thus, as Mr. Evans reminds us, a British coin, whose obverse was a much degraded form of the type of our Pl. VIII., No. 19, so that it had come to represent merely a series of irregular bands of various thickness, was interpreted by a Mr. Borlase as giving the plan of a city, and Mr. Polwhele, not to be outdone, identified the city as Exeter, protesting that no one who had visited the latter place could fail in recognising the plan of it upon the British coin.[1] In similar fashion the well-known *Tours* type (see Part 2), which is simply a transformation of the temple in the *Xristiana Religio* type of Louis the Pious, has been interpreted as the ground plan of the town of Tours; a map of Saxon London has been discovered on a small Saxon gold coin, and the plan of the gardens of Alcinous (by a more pardonable error[2]) has,

[1] Evans, *Coins of the Ancient Britons*, p. 82.

[2] As there are two undoubted instances of ground plans (real or fanciful) on Greek coins—the harbour of Zancle and the labyrinth of Crete.

even by the famous Eckhel, been made out of a simple floral pattern on the coins of Corcyra.[3]

I do not think that we are, even at the present day, quite above the possibility of errors similar in kind if less in magnitude than these. And one way of avoiding them will be found in keeping constantly in view what in the sense of the present essay I may call the *morphological* aspect of the coin-type. Wherefore, if this study is in the strictest sense rather an anthropological than a numismatic one (bearing to Numismatics, perhaps, something of the relation which Botany bears to Horticulture), these considerations will, I hope, afford a sufficient excuse for publishing it in the pages of the Numismatic Chronicle.

The functional history of coins is the history of their changes of form, so far as these are dictated by the special function which a coinage has to perform, viz., to serve as a medium of exchange. We might at the first moment be inclined to suppose that so far as regards their currency the weight and metal were the only essential elements in the coin: but we should be in error. Though the weight and metal are essential to the existence of a coin, they cannot in themselves determine its form or its type, and that the lump of metal should have some defined form or some defined mark impressed upon it is necessary to its being a coin. The difference between exchange by weight of metal and exchange by coinage is easy to grasp: it depends entirely upon the question whether a reference to the scales or the crucible is necessary before each operation. Were men's muscles sufficiently delicate they would be able to determine the exact weight of the piece of metal merely by holding the coin in their hands. But

[3] Percy Gardner, *Floral Patterns on Arch. Gr. Coins, Num. Chron.* 1881, p. 1.

no one ever heard of such a developed sense of weight. It is much more easy to imagine a people with touch fine enough to ascertain the *volume* of the metal if the *shape* remained constant. For the mass of mankind, however, it is neither sensitiveness to weight nor to volume that is relied upon, but simply likeness in *appearance*, so that when the scales and the crucible are neither of them brought into requisition it is the eye which is relied on. The shape and general *look* of the coin are in their way quite as important elements in its morphology as what is numismatically called the type. Both shape and type are no more than the visible signs of those hidden qualities (true weight, unalloyed metal) which give the coin its actual value; and it need not be said that they are often very far from truly representing those qualities. The various ways and degrees in which those symbols of value do duty in the eyes of the users of money constitute the history of the morphology of coins. From the human side it forms a chapter of human psychology, but from the side of the piece of metal it is simply a chapter in natural evolution.

There is one important fact connected with their morphology whereby coins are, so far as I can at present see, distinguished from almost all the other implements used by mankind, and in this respect rendered specially interesting subjects for this sort of study. They follow a law of heredity—as we may fairly call it—only less constant than the law of heredity in organic life. Almost all implements do in fact bow to a similar law, but it is in their case only established *ex post facto;* in the case of coins it must be laid down as a necessary principle. Thus it is a *fact* that each sword or plough or water-jar is shaped essentially upon the pattern of the sword or plough or water-jar which was in use before it. But there is no absolute reason in the nature of things why some heaven-sent genius should not at once invent the ideal or perfect type of each. Each has a definite function to perform: find out the best material for performing that function, the best way of shaping that material, and the thing is made. But coins have to perform no special function in relation to natural forces. Their concern is chiefly with human character: they have to pass current as media of exchange. Their capacity of so passing current is determined, at least so far as the form of coins is concerned, by men's familiarity with the previous issue. Each issue, therefore, must by its very function inherit something from the issue which preceded it. It would be out of the power of any single person or any historical event wholly to revolutionise a coinage. I must in honesty confess that in one or two cases the likeness between the parent species and the derived species is very faint, far fainter than are the traces of descent in the history of most implements not governed by the same necessary law. This is due to the exceedingly advanced stage of civilisation to which coins as a class belong, whereas the history of the evolution of other implements takes its most striking illustrations from days of a very primitive civilisation. The causes of variation in coins which fight against the law of heredity and produce varieties or fresh species, are, of course, very numerous; the religious, the artistic, and the historical can, however, be signalised as the chief. By the first the coinage of any people is subjected to their special religious opinions. The most striking example (as we shall see anon) of the influence of this motive is to be found in the Mohammedan coinage. The artistic and historical instincts produce the two qualities which collectors most prize in coins—their worth as art treasures and their antiquarian value. These three forms of selection—religious, artistic, and historical—we will distinguish as x, y, z, and in order to save space, any one of those letters placed in brackets after an example of morphology must be taken to imply a reference to this passage.

This paper is written chiefly to emphasize the law of heredity in coin-types, and to illustrate this law, not merely by selected examples but throughout all the most important varieties of coinage in the greater portion of the globe. Taking the larger divisions of numismatics, as Greek, Roman, Arabic, Indian, Mediæval, &c., to form the *orders* in which the coins (as natural products) are classed, the succession of each new dynasty may be said generally to give us a new *species* of coin. The *stamp* (type or inscription) being the official guarantee to which the coin owes its very existence, the species changes when some violent change has taken place in the governing power. Therefore, if we are attempting to establish the law of heredity throughout one vast genus of coins, we require first to establish that law at the point of transition from one species to another. And it is to these links only that I shall call the attention of the reader in the present paper. Even here it has been necessary to leave out of account those cases in which the chain seemed obviously unbroken, as, for example, throughout nearly the whole of the Greek autonomous coinage, in the transition from the Roman family issues to the Roman imperial coinage, most of the Mohammedan currencies, and numerous changes of dynasty which took place, between the introduction of the Carlovingian *denarius* and the reintroduction of a gold coinage, in Western Europe. Thus, the illustrations at the end are not designed to show the processes of descent and variation where these are most conspicuous, but, on the contrary, only the connecting links between the different species of coins at the very point where these are *weakest*. For want of space, too, it has been impossible in most cases to show more than one stage of transition. When, therefore, one illustrated coin is spoken of as derived from another it is rarely the case that the immediate parentage and childhood are shown; there are almost always finer stages of transition than can be given in the illustrations. I am aware that this method of treatment will produce a certain disappointing effect on any one who has no knowledge of coins. If I had chosen only one or two phases of the evolution of coins and illustrated these with tolerable fulness, the effect to the eye would have been much more satisfying, but that would have been inconsistent with the plan of the present article, which must, after all, be looked upon only as a rough preliminary sketch and an introduction to the study of coin-morphology.

Though we are chiefly concerned with the direct descent of the species of coins we shall see incidentally some other applications of morphological law. And in fact the examples of morphology will tend to group themselves into the following three classes.

A. We have first the simple law of descent whereby the form (shape, type, &c., colour even, being all considered as elements in this form) of each species is to a great extent determined by the form of the preceding species. Incidentally we shall also come to notice (*a*) how very few (comparatively speaking) are the examples of really original *types* on coins, and (*b*) how little changes of dynasty seem as a rule to affect the morphology of coins, a fact which suggests that conquests and changes of dynasty have less effect upon the domestic conditions of a people than historians are wont to imagine.

B. There is further a noticeable likeness between all the coins circulating among people who have pretty close commercial relations, and it is to be presumed pretty close relations of all kinds. There is at the present day, for example, a general likeness in all the coins which pass current in Europe, the coins of Turkey diverging the farthest from the common standard; and the divergence in this case being a fair index of divergence on other points. As a rule this class resemblance depends upon the simple law of inheritance; in other words, on the copying of one species by another. In the example given we shall see better presently that the divergence mainly depends on this law. But it will be impossible in the course of this inquiry to trace the pedigree of every member of a class which gives examples of this kind of analogous variation. When, for instance, through a multiform series of Greek coins we see the gradual elimination of the incuse square going on side by side in the coinages of different cities, it is enough to indicate such a change as an example under class B.

C. Thirdly, there is the peculiar sort of morphology shown when a barbarous or semi-barbarous people, incapable of inaugurating or much modifying a coinage of its own, takes as a model the money of some other state and makes either imitations or reproductions of it in a descending order of degradation. The examples of this class C take generally one of two forms:—*a.* If the nation is not very barbarous it sometimes invents for itself a new type founded upon the parent type, and adheres to that for a long succession of years. Such people are not artistic enough or original enough to produce variations of importance on this fixed type. *b.* A much more barbarous people, who are incapable of either inventing any type for themselves or of copying correctly that which is before them, produce a series of successive degradations which are very curious and interesting to trace. For a typical example of C *a* we may take the Parthian coinage. The typical examples of C *b* are the Gaulish or British series.

The more barbarous the copy, the greater generally is the importance attributed to the type. Perhaps the supreme instance of such barbarous copying is the example given in the last Plate of an imitation of a Venetian sequin made apparently for currency in North Africa. The copy here has given up everything but a faint resemblance of type. It is simply a piece of copper, not bearing in metal or weight the remotest likeness to the gold coin of which it is an imitation. It is indeed possible that the piece in question may have been designed for use only as a charm, not as a medium of exchange. But from the number and the similarity of the pieces which have come into my hands, I think this was not the case.

In noting during the following rapid sketch the different examples of coin-change the letters A (or A *a*, A *b*) B, C (C *a*, C *b*) will show to which of the above three classes any example is to be referred.

The idea of a coinage has been independently evolved in two places upon the earth's surface, and, so far as we can tell, in two only. In the West it was invented in Lydia early in the seventh century B.C. In the far East it was invented in China (probably) about the same time.[4] The examples given are confined altogether to the first family or *genus*. The second has scarcely yet received in any published work a complete and scientific arrangement, and if it had I am too completely ignorant of the coinage to dare to study the sequence of its types. In

[4] Prof. T. de LaCouperie informs me that metal implements were long current in China merely as media of exchange. Some of the examples which we possess of a date as early as

some coins of the regions where these two *genera* meet we can clearly trace this influence of a double descent (*e. g.* Tibet, Nepál—English coins of China and Japan).

The coinage of the West begins with the small stamped ingots of impure gold (electrum) which were first issued by the Mermnadæ kings of Lydia at the beginning of the seventh century, and which were speedily imitated by the Greek cities nearest to Lydia, those of the coast and islands of Asia Minor. The whole class is known under the name of the early electrum staters. The very earliest of these pieces have no distinguishing type, but only a punch-mark to show that they might be accepted as currency without reference to the scales. This punch-mark, therefore, is the final element which differentiates these earliest coins from the class of mere lumps of metal. A type was soon added upon the other side, but for a long time afterwards the punch or anvil mark remained upon one side of the coin, and for some while it continued to be in a morphological sense more distinctly the *type* of the coinage than the design which was added afterwards as an ornament to the piece; so that wider relationships of these archaic coins can be traced by observing the form of the incuse marking than any discoverable by observing the designs (numismatically termed the *types*) alone. But as might be expected in the case of pieces of metal which had only just emerged from the condition of being current by weight only, neither sort of type takes a very important place. There was no time for men through a long course of years to become familiarised with and attached to any particular type. The electrum staters and the archaic silver coins

B.C. 1000, are so thin that they could never have been intended for use. In the middle of the seventh century we have pieces of the same kind with an official stamp, and therefore we may fairly say, converted into coins.

most nearly related to them are, however, all distinguished by a peculiarity of form, being of an oval or bean shape, a class familiar enough to the numismatist, and of which examples are given in Pl. VIII., Nos. 1—3 (A). As might be expected, this bean shape lingered longest in the district where it had been first introduced (A). Farther to the East again the electrum staters gave rise to the Persian *darics*, first coined by Darius Hystaspides, about B.C. 516 (No. 2) (B), which subsequently, in the absence of a native Greek gold coinage, served the purpose of an international currency among the Greeks. On this account, but partly also because it arose among a people less artistically cultivated than the Greeks (C *a*), the daric had to become stereotyped, and remained so throughout the whole after history of the Achæmenian dynasty, so that when Alexander the Great continued the issue of these *darics* he had to repeat the archaic type which had been introduced nearly two centuries before. The silver pieces (*sigloi*) which were copied from the darics form another member of this earliest class of coins.

In the West (Greece proper) the eldest descendant of the staters of Asia Minor is the silver coinage of Ægina (A) (silver always obtaining in Greece proper as the national currency, and probably having been the standard medium long before it was ever *coined*, when ἀργύριον came to stand for *money* generally). The early Æginetan coins preserve something of the bean shape derived from the Lydian coinage (No. 3). From this currency are in turn descended the two most important silver coinages of Greece, the Athenian and the Corinthian (A) (Pl. VIII., Nos. 4, 7, 10, 13). It is well known that the Æginetan coins formed the currency of Athens down to the time of Solon's *seisachtheia* (when both type and weight standard were changed (*z*)) but that from that time they became so unpopular as to be hardly even mentionable. People may disown, but it is impossible for them to destroy, their parentage, and the shape and general appearance of the Athenian coins (some, as No. 4, have the bean shape) sufficiently attest their origin.

It has been already hinted that in connecting one sub-species of these archaic Greek coins with another, the shape of the incuse mark is sometimes a better guide than the type. The very earliest electrum coins have an oblong sinking between two smaller square ones as in No. 1. The next form (apparently) is that of two squares (or approximate squares) of different sizes side by side or joined together. We may imagine this formed by the uniting of the oblong incuse of the first type with one of the squares at the side. This form again (we are still among the electrum class) changes into two equal squares, or into two equal oblongs, according to the influence of the earlier or later forms. On the silver coins of Greece proper the two squares have coalesced into one, which is, however, divided by several cross lines. The cross lines become regular perpendicular and diagonal lines (as in our Union Jack), and, anon, some of the incuse sinkings being filled up, we get the windmill incuse, which characterizes a large number of archaic coins. (Cf. Nos. 3, 7, and 9; in the latter two, the windmill incuse may be said to be in process of formation.) In one special case the windmill incuse developes, under artistic influence (*y*), into the swastika-shape given on No. 10, a coin of Corinth, but of a later date than No. 7. These stages and other changes of form mark the descent of the second great international Greek currency, the coinage of Corinth.

The coinages of Athens and of Corinth became, we have said, the international silver currencies of the Greeks. Compared with them the local issues of different cities may be regarded as a kind of token money not acceptable, except by weight, outside a narrow area. Of course in the case of these again there were great differences in the area over which they had currency, the coinages of the Bœotian and the Achæan confederations coming next to those of Athens and Corinth in this respect. But on the present occasion we will neglect all but the two principal currencies. On account of the wide acceptance of the Athenian and Corinthian coins their types became much more fixed than in the case of the lesser States, and of these the Athenian more so than the Corinthian, and for this reason:—the coins of Athens circulated eastward among the people who knew not the Greeks and required a permanent guarantee of genuineness (C). The coinage of Corinth circulated westward among the Greek colonists of the Mediterranean, who would not be startled by any moderate change. The example most frequently quoted to show the necessity of a permanent type for currency among remote or half-civilised people is the experience of our invasion of Abyssinia in 1867-8, when it was found that Maria Theresa dollars were the only coins readily accepted by the natives of that country, and our government was obliged to request the government of Austria to coin us a number of such pieces from the old dies. Perhaps the relative position of the Corinthian and Athenian coinages may be better illustrated by the case of two cotton manufacturers, one of whom has a home market and the other a market chiefly in India. To the latter his Trade Mark is a matter of supreme importance, he cannot change or modify it, and any colourable imitation might be most injurious to his trade; and as a fact firms in this position have been ready to expend immense sums in defending their trade marks from imitation. From the point of view of our present study, the same process may be described as the fixing of a chance variety by its removal into a suitable environment, by removing it from the operation of those varying influences which were spoken of above. The kind of selection of which the coinage of Corinth had to take account arose mainly from the growing artistic instincts of the Greek peoples among whom these pieces were current, and who, it may be presumed, would not willingly have tolerated any rude or archaic coinage when they had developed such beautiful coinages of their own (*y*). Accordingly the money of Corinth is a compromise between the permanence necessary to satisfy the commercial and the development requisite to satisfy the artistic instincts of the Greeks.

We will now glance at the chief descendants of each series in succession. The Athenian coinage obtained a currency far away in the East, and pieces have, I believe, been discovered even on the banks of the Indus. Barbarous imitations, too, of Athenian coins have been found in Bactria and Ariana (C *b*). But the most notable route along which the Attic coins passed, giving rise where they travelled to an imitative currency, was through Gaza, in the south of Palestine, into Southern Arabia. At first the coins used in these places were of the genuine Attic coinage, but when, at the end of the fifth century (owing to the decay of Athens) this supply was stopped, imitations in various degrees of barbarism followed, both in the town of Gaza itself and among the Arabs of South Arabia. Such barbarous imitations of Athenian tetradrachms of the earlier and later style made in Southern Arabia we give in Pl. VIII., Nos. 5 and 6.[5]

---

[5] For a fuller account of these imitations see *Num. Chron.* 1877, p. 221, &c., J. P. Six, *Monnaies Phéniciennes* (*Gaza*). *Ibid.* 1878, p. 273, B. V. Head, *Himyarite and other Arabian imitations of coins of Athens.* G. Schlumberger, *Le Trésor de San'á*, 1880. *Num. Chron.* 1880, B. V. Head, *On a Himyaritic tetradrachm and the* Trésor de San'á.

The Corinthian coins, which more nearly resemble the early Æginetan than the Athenian, become differentiated from them by their increasing flatness and thinness, thus more and more departing from the thick bean shape of the *electrum staters*, the *darics* and *sigloi*. As we travel farther to the West we see this characteristic flatness more and more emphasized, until we arrive at those very peculiar flat archaic coins which are characteristic of Italy (cf. No. 8—Metapontum). Influenced solely by morphological appearances, I should not have hesitated to point to No. 9 (Selinos) as a transitional type. It is not less characteristic of a class of archaic Sicilian coins (Himera, Zancle) than the coin of Metapontum is characteristic of a certain series of Italian archaic coins (Tarentum, Poseidonia, Sybaris, Caulonia, Croton, &c.).

But it is not considered probable by those who have a special knowledge of this branch of Numismatics, to whom I have referred this question, that there was an intermediate type between the Corinthian and the flat archaic Italian type of coin. We must therefore look upon this special instance of transition as more rapid than usual. The relationship of the Sicilian archaic coins to the Corinthian is much more obvious. Selinos is the example which I have chosen, because on various grounds (weight-standard, the antiquity of the remains from the city, &c.) it seems the natural one to assume as the direct offspring of the coinage of Corinth: Zancle and Himera, and after them Naxos, may have adopted their coins from Selinos. The earliest coinage of Syracuse (in spite of the importance of this city) must be later in date than the coinages which we have just named. But the earliest Syracusan coins have in some points a specially strong resemblance to the coinage of Zancle (Messana). The relationship of the Syracusan to the Corinthian coinage cannot be further examined here, but before we leave the subject we must notice the important new species which sprang out of this particular class —the Siculo-Punic coins, namely, giving rise in their turn to the pure Carthaginian coinage of type Nos. 11, 12.[6]

No. 13 shows the second type of Corinthian coinage when the head of Pallas replaces the old incuse marking. In this we see the beginning of the elimination of the incuse square. In No. 14, a later Corinthian coin, this process is complete.

From the Greek it is easy to trace the development of the Græco-Italian coinage, and from that of the earliest silver currency of Rome. Two stages in this evolution are represented on the plate, No. 15 being a Campanian coin current in Rome before the regular series of Roman family coins begins, and No. 16 being the obverse of the earliest type of Roman silver coins. This is enough to connect the Roman coinage and all its derivatives with the series which we have at present in hand. Of the exact relationship of the Roman and the Greek coinages we will speak again when we come to treat the Roman as the head of a new family of coinages.

The next sub-species which we will select out of the whole species of Greek coins, is the gold coinage of Philip of Macedon, which for the first time supplied the Greeks with a national gold currency of native origin (No. 17). This is the first Greek coinage which had a great and immediate influence in giving rise to barbaric types of money. "The stater of Philip—the *regale numisma* of Horace—became everywhere diffused, and seems at once to

[6] An excellent example of a Carthaginian coin debased from the Syracusan obverse and the Syracusan-Corinthian reverse, is given in B. M. Guide (Head, Pl. 59, No. 35).

have been seized upon by the barbarians who came in contact with Greek civilisation as an object of imitation. In Gaul this was especially the case, and the whole of the gold coinage of that country may be said to consist of imitations more or less rude and degenerate of the Macedonian *philippus*."[7] No. 18 (obverse only) is a specimen of a Gaulish or somewhat early imitation of No. 17 (C *b*). A whole series of pieces might be chosen to show the gradual degeneration of the type, as also its further degradation in the hands of the Britons who copied from the Gaulish money (C *b*.) No. 19 (obverse and reverse) is a British coin. But the subject has been so completely worked out by Mr. Evans in the book referred to, that it needs only to be touched upon here. Sometimes classed with the Gaulish coins is a series of pieces rather peculiar in type, and belonging apparently to the region of Pannonia. Among the German peasantry the coins have acquired the name of *Regenbogenschüsseln*, from the superstition that they are actual specimens of "rainbow gold." They have more than once been made the subject of special monographs.[8] These we must also count among the barbaric descendants of the Macedonian *philippus* (C *b*), far removed as they seem at first sight from their prototypes. Among the silver Gaulish coins which had a greater diversity of origin, it will be enough here to notice Nos. 21, 22, descended from the coinage of the Spanish colony of Rhoda,[9] No. 20 (C *b*).

A universal currency—not only for Greece in the nar-

---

[7] Evans, *Coins of the Anc. Brit.*, p. 24.

[8] Streber, *Regenbogenschüsseln;* Friedländer in *Bullettino di Arch.*; *Rev. Num.* 1861, p. 141 (Longpérier).

[9] *Rev. Num.* 1866, p. 389 (L. de la Saussaye); *Ibid.* 1867, p. 1 (F de Saulcy).

rower sense, but for that Greater Hellas in the East which was created by this conqueror—was instituted by Alexander the Great. Of all the pieces of Alexander, the most characteristic and the most influential in determining the future forms of the coinage were his tetradrachms, which, so far as they themselves had a distinct parentage, must be affiliated to the tetradrachms of Athens, which at an earlier period had enjoyed so wide a circulation, and whose place the tetradrachms of Alexander were designed to supply.[10] A specimen of the Alexandrine tetradrachms is given on Pl. IX., No. 23. On the obverse the head of young Heracles, which, after the death of Alexander, gradually merges into the head of Alexander himself: on the reverse a seated Zeus holding the eagle. This reverse type is replaced sometimes on the coins of Alexander's successors (without changing essentially the appearance of the coin) by a seated Pallas Athene. The Alexandrine tetradrachms are the immediate parents of several distinct series of coins which arose under the successors of Alexander in the different territories which he conquered. From the veiled portraiture of the Macedonian coins we pass to the unabashed portraiture of the Ptolemies and the Seleucidæ, and of the lesser kingdoms which took their cue from them. Of these various series the coins of the Seleucids (kings of Syria and a portion of Asia Minor) are the most interesting for the present study (Nos. 24, 25). While appropriately to the soil upon which they found themselves, the coins of the kings of Egypt (the Ptolemies) became absolutely stereotyped, the coins of the Seleucidæ expanded into so many varieties as almost to form a new species. Each succeeding monarch placed his own portrait

---

[10] See Müller, *Numis. d'Alexandre le Grand.* Planches.

upon his own coinage, and the reverse types, though constantly recurring, are likewise very numerous. Let No. 24 serve as a general specimen of the class and show its relationship to the coinage of Alexander. Of the varieties of Seleucid coins No. 25 is, so far as regards the class to which it belongs, one of the least important. It is a coin of Antiochus II., called Theos. The reverse type shows Apollo seated on the *omphalos,* holding out a bow in his right hand, and resting his left hand on the omphalos on which he sits. A similar seated figure of Apollo is very common on the Seleucid coins. But generally the god holds out an *arrow* or *arrows* in his *right* hand, and with his *left* leans upon the *bow,* which touches the ground. This special variety is only found on the money of Antiochus II. and of Antiochus Hierax.[11] If we had no historical information as to the date of the Parthian revolt[12] we should be able to determine it with considerable exactitude. For it is from this special variety of the Seleucid coinage that the new Parthian, or let us rather say Arsacid, series is derived (No. 26) (C *a*). At a first glance it might appear as if the Parthian coinage was a really original type, seeing that the figures on either side are Parthian figures and wear the Parthian cap or helmet. But a moment's comparison with the Seleucid coinage shows us how unoriginal the type is.

The Parthian coin is not a slavish imitation of the Seleucid, and therefore it is an example of class C *a*. The head of Antiochus Theos gives place to the head of the Parthian King, or what is meant for that, and the same

---

[11] Gardner, *Cat. of Coinage of the Seleucidæ*, pp. 8, 20.

[12] The probable date of it is B.C. 249. See Gardner i[illegible] [illegible] *Orient.*, *Parthian Coinage*, p. 3.

personage replaces Apollo on the reverse—"the religious character of Greek coins," about which so much has been written, not holding when we come to Parthia. And yet we observe that the attitude of the reverse figure, the arrangement of the legend,[13] &c., are so exactly alike on both coins that not a doubt could exist that one is the prototype of the other. We observe that the head on one side and the figure on the other have been both turned round from right to left, as would necessarily happen if the artist copied upon his die the prototype just as he saw it. It is so often that types are reversed by this process (of copying what is seen upon the die) that in finding out a prototype it is often a guide to us to observe that the type has been reversed. The more barbarous the copy, as a general rule, the more likely is this change to have taken place. The Parthian coinage is not a barbarous one of the same kind as the Gaulish and British series; but it is still barbarous enough to be without the changing influence of art, which has such a powerful effect in varying the types of Greek coins. And, in fact, throughout the whole region of coin-morphology there are few better examples to be found of the conversion of a chance variety into a new species by transplantation to a soil where it was freed from the influences which would have changed the type in its original country (Nos. 26—28). Later on we get some instances of the wholly barbaric style in the Parthian coinage.[14] (No. 28, reverse; C *b.*)

[13] A form of selection comes in, in one respect, and affects the length of the legend on the reverse. The legend increases successively from two to three, four and five lines under the influence of the vanity of the Arsacid kings, who were continually adding to the titles on their coins.

[14] See also Gardner, *op. cit.*, pl. vii., Nos. 15, 19, 20, for examples of still further degradation.

Now that we are fully started upon this line of descent we will follow it to the end. The next step is the transition from the Parthian to the Sassanian coinage. As the Sassanian dynasty immediately (by conquest) succeeded to the Parthian in Persia, we might expect that the line of demarcation between the two coinages would be very fine. This is not the case taking them all together. The example given in Pl. IX. No. 29—a coin of the first Sassanian King Artaxerxes or Ardeshir I. (A.D. 235)—is indeed a close copy of No. 27, which is a Parthian coin. But the latter is of Sinatruces,[15] who flourished about B.C. 77, or three hundred years before the Sassanian King. Such an instance of copying is rather opposed to than in accordance with the ordinary laws of morphology. It is as important to take account of such abnormal specimens as of the normal ones. There would, however, be no difficulty in showing, by grouping together a number of examples, that the ordinary Sassanian coin-types are descended somewhat irregularly from the Parthian coin-types [16] (Nos. 28, 30). The disturbing, or, as we have sometimes called them, the *selecting*, influences of art and religion are, however, very apparent in the Sassanian coinage. The Sassanian kings were not only passionate revivalists of the older Magism, but were likewise revivers of no small portion of the art of the Achæmenian days. And it is very easy to see by a comparison between the portraits of the kings on the Sassanian coins and those on the Sassanian monuments

---

[15] The prototype of No. 29 is probably, too, a similar coin of Mithradates I., who preceded Sinatruces by seventy years, the coinage of this great conqueror being much more extensive than that of his successor.

[16] Compare Gardner, *Parthian Coins*, pl. vii., with Thomas, *Sassanian Coins*, pl. iii., esp. G. vii. 13, 14, with T. 1, G. vii. 5, 6, &c., with T. 3.

(Texier, plates) that the art of the former is essentially national (*x*, *y*, *z*). The fire-altar, again, which appears in one shape or another on nearly all the Sassanian coins, is an original type, and due to the religious revivalism of the Sassanian kings. On the whole, therefore, though this case comes under the head of class A, the disturbing or selecting influences (*x*, *y*, *z*) are too numerous to make the Sassanian coinage a good example of the law of heredity. It forms rather than otherwise an exception to class A *b*. On the same line of descent we now come to a far more interesting instance. No. 30 is a Sassanian coin of the usual later type. The fire-altar with its two supports has developed into a taller altar with a figure standing on either side.[17] What is peculiar to the later coin is its breadth and flatness, different from anything which had been known in the earlier history of Numismatics.[18] The piece photographed is a coin of the "madman" Khusrú II. (Chosroes), who tore up Mohammed's letter of exhortation, and threw it into the Karasú,[19] and whose immediate descendants were finally overthrown by the Moslems in the series of engagements which ended in the great battle of Nehávend, A.D. 641. When the Arab Khalif of Damascus (the first dynasty, the descendants of Omeyyah) established a coinage of their own, they modelled their silver currency upon the Sassanian money, and this first coinage of the Ommeyads was the parent of all the numberless varieties of Mohammedan coins.

Look at the reverse of No. 33 from a little distance

---

[17] The process can be traced in Mordtmann, *Münzen mit Pehlvi-Legenden*. Taf. vi. 3, 4, 79.

[18] Characteristics which unfortunately cannot be adequately shown by the photographs.

[19] Gibbon (ed. Smith), v. p. 395, *note* (Milman).

beside the reverse of No. 30, and they seem almost identical in form. Looking closer we see that one consists of two figures and a fire-altar between them, and an inscription round; the type of the other is entirely made up of inscriptions, the figures and fire-altar have been replaced by three lines containing the grand Mohammedan formula—

لا اله الا	There is no God but
الله وحده	God. He is alone.
لا شريک له	There is no companion to Him.

The earlier coin has a Pehlvi legend. It is here replaced by one in Arabic, but of course the grand change is that which is due to Mohammed's prohibition of the representation of all living things (x).[20] No. 33 was struck at Damascus only seventy-nine years after the Flight (only sixty after the battle of Nehávend)—almost the earliest genuinely Mohammedan coin which exists.[21] The stern rule of the Prophet has stepped in and introduced for the first time in the coinage of the Western *genus* a piece of money devoid of any representation. But it has not been able for all that to break through the law of heredity. We observe how the marginal circles have been preserved almost intact, and how the crescents and stars on one coin have changed to corresponding annulets on the other.

We are not here concerned with history, but with morphology only. We will therefore still linger for a

---

[20] *Cat. Or. Coins, Br. Mus.* (S. Lane-Poole), vol. i., pl. i. and ii. No. 32, struck at Tabaristan contemporarily with the beginning of the Khalifate, may be a transition type between 30 and 33.

[21] Very few Ommeyad coins exist of a date earlier than A.H. 76.

few moments over this line of descent in order to dismiss, as we shall be obliged to do in a few paragraphs, the vast Mohammedan coinage, of which we have just shown the origin. This immense class, distinguished as we have said from almost all the other species of Western origin by its want of figure-types, yet shows such varieties in the arrangement of its inscriptions as to form for the morphologist a series of different types or sub-species, which the practised eye can at once recognise. In most cases the descent of the coins of one dynasty from those of another is an instance of direct inheritance, coming under class A. Even so it is very interesting to see how slight varieties gradually sprang up, and in their turn got transmitted by inheritance, and a minute study of the descent of the Arab coins would repay the student. But with the numerous species of coin which still remain unmentioned, I must leave the detailed study of this particular one to others, and not attempt it in the present instance. It is enough to show the general lines upon which our route would carry us. Thus, having found the origin of the coins of the first dynasty (Ommeyads), the descent from these of the coins of the second dynasty (the 'Abbáside Khalifs of Bagdad) is plain enough.[22] There the first faint varieties begin to appear. The divergence is greater between the 'Abbásí coins and those of the Ommeyad Khalifs of Cordova, which have also for their parents the Ommeyads of Damascus.[23] The peculiarities of the coins of the Khalifs of Cordova are emphasized in the lesser dynasties which sprang up on the decay of this Khalifate.[24] The characteristic features of the 'Abbásí coins are on the other hand best preserved in

---

[22] *Cat. Or. Coins* (B.M.), vol. i., pl. iii. *sq.*
[23] *Op. cit.* vol. ii.
[24] *Op. cit.* vol. ii.

coinages which sprang up on quite the opposite side of the Mohammedan world of that date, in Persia, namely, Mesopotamia and Transoxiana[25] (Samánís, Hamdánís, Buweyhís). All the series hitherto spoken of have been founded on the *silver* coins of the Ommeyads or 'Abbásís.[26] But in Africa the dynasty of the Aghlabís founded theirs in the gold currency of the 'Abbásís (the Aghlabí *silver* coins are imitated from the Aghlabí gold). From the Aghlabite are descended the Fátimite coins.[27] In this (Fátimite) dynasty we see the spontaneous development of a new variety—coins which have their inscriptions arranged in a series of concentric circles (Pl. IX. No. 34), and this variety is handed on to the next dynasty, the Ayyúbite (A *b*). The Ayyúbite coins again change their character, and the later specimens of them are hardly distinguishable from the earliest money of the Memlúks (A *b*).[28] A more important variation than that introduced by the Fátimís is the practice of enclosing the legend within a square compartment. We have seen how the peculiar type of the Sassanian coins dictated the square form in which the legend should be written on the earliest Ommeyad coins, and this square form among the characteristic features throughout the Arab coinage is very obstinately adhered to. The notion of enclosing this legend in a compartment is a natural one, and I am not able to say where it originated, for about the beginning of the sixth century A.H. we see it coming into use at the two opposite extremities of the Muslim

---

[25] *Op. cit.* vol. ii.

[26] The Arab gold coins are in their very origin hybrids. They are in part the offspring of the solidus of Heraclius (see Part 2).

[27] *Op. cit.* vol. iv.

[28] *Op. cit.* vol. iv.

world. It is a noticeable feature in the coins of three great dynasties, the Ayyúbís, the Seljúkís (No. 35), and the Hulágúis [29] or Mongols of Persia (No. 36)—the third probably adopting it from the second. Nos. 35, 36 show the great likeness between some of the coins of the Seljúks and those of the Mongols. Many other sorts of compartments, star-shapes, six or eight foils, &c., are found in both the Ayyúbite and in the Hulágúide coins. From the Hulágúide coins are descended an immense series of coinages of the different Mongolian dynasties, descendants of Jingis Khán, and ending with the famous dynasty of Tímúr (No. 37).

In another way the Seljúks of Anatolia took a new and most important departure, namely, by neglecting the Mohammedan precept directed against the making of images. This was probably due to their contact with the Christian races in Syria and Asia Minor. But this series of image coins, in which the Seljúks were supported by a few other dynasties—Ayyúbite, Ortokite, Zengide, &c. —belongs chiefly to the classes descended from a Byzantine source, and hence to our second division, the Roman Family.

The introduction of the *tughrá* [30] or curiously interlaced monogram of the Sultan's name, with which we are familiar on modern Turkish coins (No. 38), is another curious variety. It is confined to the money of the 'Othmanli dynasty in Turkey and its provinces, and to that of the Kháns of the Crimea.[31]

Finally, in taking leave of the Arabic series we must

---

[29] *Op. cit.* vols. iii., iv., vi.

[30] *Op. cit.* vol. viii.

[31] *Op. cit.* vol. vi., p. 197, pl. viii. *Khans of the Crimea.* There is a figure which might be called a *tughrá* on some modern coins of Afghanistán.

notice how completely the style and general appearance of the Western coinages differ from the class which was developed east of the Indus. From the time of the Afghan conquerors of Delhi down to the modern *rupí*, there is a traceable sequence with certain main characteristics of thickness and general solidity which contrasts altogether with all other series of Arab coins, tracing their descent from the thin coins of the Sassanians. It is impossible to show this difference in a photograph, but anyone who has handled a native rupí and a modern Turkish or Egyptian coin will be sensible of the difference—still more sensible if the coin in each case be about a hundred years old (No. 38). The coinage of the present Persian dynasty, the Sefevis, is founded upon the Indian pattern, so that of the present two great coinages of the Moslem world, the Turkish and the Persian Mohammedan, one represents the true, and the other the Indo-Arabic, Mohammedan series. It would not be too much to say that the one derives its type originally from the Sassanian, and the other from the Bactrian coinage.

To the Bactrian coinage we now turn. It begins about the same time as the Parthian series, and, like it, it is derived from the money of the Seleucidæ. Here, again, a study of the types of the coinage, without any help from history, would enable us to say that the Bactrian revolt took place about the reign of the Seleucid King, Antiochus II. For the earliest Bactrian coins, those of Diodotus I., have a reverse type which is peculiar to this Antiochus. It is Zeus standing, holding the ægis and hurling a thunderbolt. The characteristic type of the coins of Euthydemus, successor to Diodotus, is Heracles seated upon a rock resting his club upon another point of rock in front of him (Pl. X., No. 39). And of this type we have many barbarous imitations of a later date. Of these one is given in the plate, No. 40.

No essential change takes place in the Indo-Bactrian coinage, though the style of it gradually deteriorates, and bilingual coins, with the legend on one side in Arian characters, and on the other in Greek, succeed the pure Greek coins. (It is worth while noticing that this change is only the *addition* of an Arian inscription to the obverse when there had been no inscription before.) But with the Indo-Scythic coinage, or, as it is sometimes called, the Mithraic, we seem to enter upon a totally new class. The exceptions to a general rule are as much worth taking account of as the cases which illustrate it, and I do not wish in any way to minimise the impression which a comparison of the Bactrian and the Mithraic coins is calculated to produce, that the latter have very few points indeed of connection with the former. The cause of this sudden new departure is believed to be the sudden influx of the Roman gold currency into India, a fact for which we have the authority of Pliny,[32] so that the Indo-Scythic coins are at least as much the descendants of the Roman aurei as of the Bactrian coins. It would not be difficult, however, to show that, so far as mere types go, the Indo-Scythic coins are largely indebted to the Bactrian (cf. Nos. 41, 42, 43). Other types, again, are derived from those on Roman coins.[33]

---

[32] Pliny, H. N. xii. 41. The weight of the Indo-Scythic gold coins is based not upon any Greek standard, but upon the weight of the Roman *aureus*. (This at least is maintained by Mr. V. Smith in J. A. S. B., vol. 53, p. 143). It may, therefore, be questioned whether this species of coin should not be referred to the Roman family rather than to the Greek.

[33] As Professor P. Gardner has in the press a catalogue of the Bactrian and Indo-Scythic coinages, which will probably be in

The first purely Indian coinage (or almost the first) is that of the Gupta kings, who seem to have ruled in the province of Benáres, though they have hitherto generally been called the Kanauj Guptas[34] (A). Here the relation between the Gupta coins and the Indo-Scythic is as close as the relation of the Indo-Scythic to the earlier Bactrian is slight and difficult to detect.[35] This series has recently been made the subject of a learned and interesting monograph by Mr. Vincent Smith, of the Bengal Civil Service. It had previously received a fair amount of rather desultory notice from Indian Numismatists, notably in the *Indian Antiquities* of Prinsep (Ed. E. Thomas), and in Wilson's *Ariana Antiqua.* The types of the Gupta coins are numerous, but we have not the least difficulty in referring the majority of them, as well as the more general type of the coinage as a whole, to the Indo-Scythic currency. And we have a series of imitations of the Mithraic coins which serve as links between the two (No. 45). The very earliest Gupta coins (those of Ghatotkacha) show on the obverse the figure of the king standing and sacrificing at a small altar, almost exactly as he stands on the *Mithraic* coins of the Indo-Scyths (cf. Nos. 44 obv. and 47 obv.; No. 45 is a transition type, a late and undetermined Mithraic coin). There is, I understand, no evidence that Ghatotkacha was a fire-worshipper, and I should think it a reasonable supposition that in adopting this type the

---

the hands of the reader not long after this essay, I will refer the reader to that book for any detailed description of the types on these coins. Probably their descent will also be there adequately traced, which could not be done here.

[34] The correction of this false localization is due to Mr. V. Smith in the paper cited above.

[35] Even this was not always acknowledged however. See Prinsep's *Indian Antiq.* ii. p. 195.

Gupta king was simply imitating as closely as possible the money which had already come into currency in his kingdom. Mr. V. Smith, indeed, sees a special meaning in this type. "I think," he says, "that it may fairly be assumed upon the evidence of the coins that Ghatotkacha (though he may have been a Hindu) was a worshipper of the solar fire, as his Indo-Scythian predecessors undoubtedly were." I do not know whether there be independent reasons for this supposition, but I venture to think that (for morphological reasons) the testimony of the coins is of very little value on this point. The figure on the *reverse* of these first Gupta coins may likewise be matched by a similar figure on the Indo-Scythic coins (No. 44 rev. and 47 rev.).

Mr. Smith has discussed with great care and learning the various types of the Gupta coins, and has classified them in a way eminently useful for study. It would not be necessary for us (and what is more to the purpose, would in our present space be quite impossible) to discuss these types in detail, seeing that the parentage of the Gupta coinage can never be called in question. One type only calls for some notice: it is that of a seated goddess. Sometimes she is upon a throne, at other times she is seated upon a peacock, more often on a lotus-flower.[36] There is some dispute about the precise nature of this goddess of the lotus-flower. Mr. Thomas says she is Párvatí, Mr. Smith that she is Lakshmí. Mr. Smith confesses that it is not very easy to determine the exact significance of any such representation. "The names and attributes of gods or goddesses in India or elsewhere," he quotes, "are all no-

[36] J. A. S. B., vol. liii., p. 120, &c. (V. Smith), pl. iii., 1, 2, 9, 10; iv. 4, 5, 7, 8, 9, 10, 11, 12, and No. 48 on our plate.

thing more than the feeble efforts of the human imagination to express by metaphor and symbol imperfectly-apprehended ideas of the attributes of the unspeakably divine nature, and it is futile to attempt to draw sharp lines of demarcation between these symbolical expressions."[37] We may add that when they were engaged in manufacturing coin types the introducers were not always even so much as attempting to express these high matters, but were often enough content to hand on some type which had become familiarised to their eyes. Thus there is no doubt that the seated goddess on the Gupta coins has its prototype on Kanerki coins of the Indo-Scythic class.[38]

The Gupta series is the beginning of a genuine Indian coinage. The series of native coins east of the Indus (except when we come to the classes whose origin was in the far East) are not numerous or important until the introduction of the Mohammedan series. Some examples of like imitations of the Indo-Scythic coins may be noticed. Of these, one is given on the Plate (No. 46). Three other series, too, are worthy of a moment's attention, and with them we come to the end of our first division, the coins directly descended from the Greek coinage.[39] These three classes are the Sáh coins of Sauráshtra, the later Guptas of the

---

[37] P. 135.

[38] Compare Nos. 45 (rev.), 48 (rev.); No. 45, as has been said, does not belong to the classified Indo-Scythic coins. But the prototype of that seated figure is common enough on genuine Indo-Scythic pieces.

[39] The descent of all these series from the Greek-Bactrian coins was long ago maintained by Prinsep. "I will appeal," he says, "solely to the close family resemblance of four distinct classes of Hindu coins, to what may be called their Bactrian prototypes; namely, those of Kanauj; the latter class of the Bihar Buddhist group; the coins of Sauráshtra and those which Stacey has denominated Rajput coins."–*Ind. Ant.* (Ed. E. Thomas), ii. p. 196.

same region, and the Rajpút coinages of Rajpútana. The first two seem to be descended from the earlier Bactrian coins. They both have the same head upon the obverse (Nos. 49, 50), and this head it is believed is derived from that of Euthydemus I., or, at any rate, of some Bactrian ruler. The reverse of the Sáh coins, the Chaitya or Buddha monument, has certainly also a prototype on Bactrian coins. But it occurs on certain transitional series closely related to the Bactrian. The Gupta coins of Saurâshtra are, I suppose, founded upon the Sáh coins. But the reverse of the majority of these pieces is derived from that very goddess on the lotus (Párvatí or Lakshmí) whom we have been discussing. The reverse of No. 50 is only a degraded form of No. 48 (rev.).[40] The same type (cf. 48) reappears on the coinage of Mohammed ibn Sám of Dehli (No. 55).

We come, finally, to the Rajpút coins (No. 53), whose types are a horseman on one side and a bull upon the other. They are generally believed to be descended from the Bactrian coins, or their Indo-Scythic descendants. As Prinsep says, "They are linked on the one hand by the subject of their impression with the Indo-Scythic series, and on the other gradually mixed with and transfused into the Arabic of the first Mohammedan conquerors of India."[41] It would not be easy to fix upon any single type from which the Rajpút coinage (No. 53) is derived. No. 51, a coin of Azes, bears a sufficiently close resemblance to No. 53, so far as mere type is concerned. But the differences of metal and shape preclude the idea of

---

[40] This descent has been developed by Thomas, *Dynasty of the Guptas*, x. p. 3. See Prinsep, vol. ii., pl. xix., Nos. 7, 15, 20, xx., No. 34, *op. cit.* p. 202 *seq.*

[41] Prinsep, ii. p. 299.

direct descent of one from the other. On the other hand, the types of the humped bull (*Bos Indicus,* or zebu, often called the Bactrian bull) is exceedingly common on both the later Bactrian and the Indo-Scythian coinages, as is the type of a horseman, who appears in both silver and copper coins, though he is never quite like the Rajpút horseman. When the Ghóris invaded India they adopted the same type upon some of their coins, and it was passed on to the first Afghan rulers of Dehli. The coin given (No. 54), on whose obverse the horseman of No. 53 can just be traced, has on the reverse the name of the Ghórí conqueror of Dehli, Mohammad Ibn Sám (13th century). No. 52 is another late (9th century) example of the Bactrian bull upon a native (non-Arabic) Indian coin.

We have now traced the principal species of coins which directly descended from the original Greek class. It will be seen that the three plates roughly correspond to three divisions of the world—Europe, Asia, with (Mohammedan) Africa, and India. Bactria belongs in the historical sequence of the coinage to both of the last two plates, and one small series of Southern Palestine and Southern Arabia is included in Pl. VIII. Among the European coin-series given on Pl. VIII., the Roman is by far the most important, becoming as it does the parent of a whole family nearly as great as that which we have just traced. Of this family we have now to speak.

Part II.[1]—The Roman Family.

In the first part of this article the Roman coinage was considered only as a single member of an immense family of coinages which could trace their descent straight back to a Greek origin. We have now to consider the Roman coinage as itself the parent of a new stock, scarcely less large in respect to the number of its members than the stock which was treated of in the first part. At the same time, we must remember that the whole family of coins derived from the Roman comes in a secondary degree within the circle of the Greek family. Before proceeding to speak of the different coinages which sprang out of the Roman, it may be as well to examine a little more closely than we were able to do in the first part the origin of the Roman money itself.

It must be remembered that the Roman coinage is not so homogeneous as the Greek. The former, after we get beyond the limits (in time and space) of the electrum staters, and before we reach those of the Macedonian stater, is essentially a currency in silver. The issues in gold or in copper are distinctly subsidiary to and dependent upon the silver coinages. But the early Roman copper coinage seems to stand apart. It is not the parent of the Roman silver coinage; nor is it, in the same sense that the silver

[1] In Part I. the references to the Plates are to the number at the top of the page; in Part II. to that at the foot.

is, a direct issue of the Greek coinage. In passing rapidly over the Roman coinage in the first part, we could only speak of the origin of the silver money. It is necessary now to say something of the origin of the copper, which was by far the most characteristic and essentially Italian of the two.

The significance of the word *æs* as the name for money generally, and in this respect the exact equivalent of the Greek ἀργύριον, is enough to show that the copper coinage of Rome was its own coinage *par excellence*. The monetary standard over the whole of Italy and in Sicily was founded upon a weight in copper, of which the units were the Roman *libra* and the Sicilian λίτρα. The process by which the currency passed by mere weight of metal—*i.e.* by unmarked blocks of copper (*æs rude*)—through the marked or *signed* masses (*æs signatum*), down to the genuine currency of the libral *as* (*æs grave*), is preserved for us in the records of finds.[2] These first Roman coins have little resemblance to any coinage current in the world at the time they were first made. They are large pieces of copper *cast* in a lenticular shape, but of an accurately circular form. It becomes a question how far they can be considered as derived from any other series, and not rather a really original coinage. The answer is that the principle of coinage was taken from the Greeks; and unless the Romans had been long familiar with the use of coins among their neighbours (both north and south), these earliest Roman coins would never have been made. The types of the earliest Roman coins—the Janus-head, the heads of Jupiter, of Hercules, of Mercury, even of Roma, and the reverse type of the prow—are, if not

---

[2] Mommsen, *Histoire de la Monn. Rom.* (Blacas tr.), i. p. 173 *seq.*

directly copied from any other coins, very obviously suggested by the Greek and Græco-Italic coinage.

In the case of the silver money, which does not begin until nearly a century after the copper coinage, the debt to the neighbouring currencies of Magna Græcia and Sicily is, as has been pointed out, very much closer. The nearest approach to the head of Roma on the Roman denarii (Pl. I. No. 16), is perhaps the helmeted head on the Campanian coin, given in Pl. I. No. 15. But other details of the head were derived from other places, as, for instance, the winged helmet from a like helmeted head of Pallas on the later coins of Metapontum and of Thurium. The descent of the type on the coinage of this last city is very curious and interesting; and perhaps, if we wanted to fix upon any one prototype of the head of Roma upon the coins of Rome, we ought to choose a very early head of Pallas on the coins of Thurium struck during the short period when the city still retained the name of its predecessor, Sybaris, *i.e.* very nearly the middle of the fifth century B.C. Pallas had in South Italy the by-name of Ρώμη (strength), and this of course would further identify her image on coins with the image of the city. The principal reverse types on the early Republican silver coins are—1. Castor and Pollux. This type, almost exactly identical with the Roman one, already existed on the silver coins of Bruttii. It is not, however, to be supposed that its adoption by the Romans was due merely to commercial considerations. The Dioscuri were specially honoured in Rome, and had been instrumental, only a few years before the introduction of a silver coinage, in gaining for them the victory of Lake Regillus, which secured them Latium.[3]

[3] Babelon, *Monnaies de la Rép. Rom.*, p. xx.

2. The type of Victory in a biga, which gained for the denarii the name of *bigati,* is also found on the coinage of Bruttii; and 3. The type of Jupiter in a quadriga (the type of the *quadrigati*) is derived from the Campanian coins.

As time goes on the two streams of the copper and silver coinages mingle more and more. The *cast* coins of the libral series, and the earlier reductions, give place soon after the introduction of a silver coinage to *struck* coins throughout the whole copper series, from the *as* to the *uncia.* And now the copper and silver run side by side through the coinage of the Republic until we get to nearly the last half century of it, when the copper coinage temporarily ceases. This brings about a general resemblance between the two series, and also a resemblance between the Roman copper coins and those of the Greek cities. The types of the Roman silver and copper remained, however, distinct throughout.

Although a gap of over half a century occurs between the later Republican and the first Roman Imperial copper coins, the latter must, I think, be reckoned as the child of the former, for a mere cessation in the striking of coins (especially when these have sunk into the class of token money) does not put them out of circulation. It is equally certain that the Roman large brass coins (so-called) are the parents of the Græco-Imperial coins, which one is justified in classing rather with the Roman series than with the Greek; on the other hand, at a later date the small brass coins (so-called), having been washed with silver and designed to pass current as denarii, belong to the silver class. The large Byzantine copper coins are apparently the legitimate offspring of the Roman large brass coins; and they, in their turn, were the progenitors of some of the large copper coins struck by the Norman dukes in South

Italy and in Sicily, and likewise by some of the Crusaders; and from the same source probably are derived the large copper coins which characterize the currencies of some few among the Tatar Mohammedan dynasties, those which come into closest contact with the Byzantine Empire—the Ayyúbis, the Urtukís, and various branches of the Bení Zengí, and other Atábegs. So we can, if we choose, trace the two separate currents in the coinage of Rome from their very sources until the fall of the Empire, and even beyond the limits of the Roman coinage.

The first coinage which began to feel the influence of Rome in an important degree was that of Gaul, which, Greek in origin, gradually changed its character until it became wholly Roman, so that the later Gaulish coinage must be reckoned in the Roman family. The same process went on, though in a less degree, in Britain. The series of coins bearing the legends COM, COM . F, TINCOM, &c., may be especially studied, in conjunction with some earlier anonymous coins from the same (south-east) district, for examples of the gradual change from a type derived originally from the Greek to a wholly Roman type.[4]

Two other series which, originally Greek, became in a large degree Romanised, were the Indo-Scythic and Gupta gold currencies, of which something has been already said. It is to Mr. Vincent Smith that we are indebted for pointing out the relationship between the weight of these pieces and that of the gold aureus; and it is to the large importation

---

[4] Evans, o. c., Pl. II., III., and Willett in *Num. Chron.*, N.S. xvii., p. 319, Pl. IX., X. (Notice especially the development of the horse from the Græco-British to the Romano-British type, Pl. IX., 1—9, 11, and Pl. IX. 10, Pl. X.)

of this latter coin that the sudden change in the character of the Indo-Scythic coinage is attributed. Previously the weight of the Indo-Scythic coins was supposed to follow, though in a degraded condition, the standard of the Macedonian gold stater.[5] Some one or two among the types in these two series may be perhaps referred to the Roman aurei. Mr. Smith indicates such points of resemblance as he believes to exist in the Gupta series. But among all the eight-and-twenty types into which he divides his Gupta coins, these traces of Roman influence are insignificant.

The real outgrowth of the descendants of the Roman coinage only begins about the time of the fall of the Empire in the West, or with the great incursions of the barbarians which marked the close of the fourth century A.D.

Of the numerous Teutonic nations which broke down the limits of the Roman Empire in the West, the most important in the formation of new kingdoms and in the issue of new series of coins were the five following:—the Vandals, the Ostrogoths, the Franks (Merovingians), the Lombards, and the Visigoths. The order in which these names are placed is the order in which we propose to consider their coinages; and the reasons for arranging them in this order will appear more clearly after that examination. It is not, of course, their proper historical sequence. The first to break the peace of the Roman Empire were the Visigoths, who in 395 revolted in the settlements of Mœsia and invaded Greece. In 400 they began, under Alaric, their invasion of Italy. But throughout this earlier portion of their career they issued no

[5] See von Sallet's papers in *Zeitschrift für Numis.*, 1879.

national coinage. It was not till they had finally settled in their homes in Spain that the Visigothic coinage began. Much the same was the case with four other barbarian nations, which, almost contemporarily with the Visigothic revolt, burst through the barriers of the Empire in the north. In 405—6 the united hordes of the Suevi, the Vandals, the Alani, and the Burgundians entered Gaul, destined never again to retreat beyond the Rhine. And this event may be reckoned the downfall of the Roman power beyond the Alps. The Burgundians alone remained in Gaul. The Suevi, Alani, and Vandals passed on into Spain, and the Vandals from Spain into Africa. The Suevi issued a short-lived coinage in the western parts of the Spanish peninsula, into which they were driven by the Visigoths. The Vandals issued an important national coinage in the African settlements in Carthago Nova for the seven provinces of Northern Africa (A.D. 484). About the same date the Franks first crossed the Rhine, and made sure their settlement in the Belgic province.

The final transfer of the power of the Western Empire to the kings of the East Goths did not take place till half a century later than the events just narrated. Romulus Augustulus was, we know, deposed by Odoacer (A.D. 476), who struck coins, interesting from their extreme rarity and for containing the first portrait upon a coin of one of the barbarian rulers who established their empire upon the fall of Rome (Pl. IV. 58). But this barbarian founded no dynasty. The definite enthronement of a race of Teutonic kings in Italy was the work of the Ostrogoths under Theodoric towards the close of the fifth century (A.D. 493). The issue of a regular Ostrogothic coinage begins with this king. The series ends with the defeat of Thila at the battle of Mons Lactarius, A.D. 553.[6] The Vandal coinage is almost contemporary with the Ostrogothic. It begins under Gunthamund, A.D. 484, and ends with the defeat of Gelimir (Geilamir) at the battle of Trikameron, A.D. 533.[7]

The coinages of the Vandals and of the Ostrogoths stand apart from all the other barbarian series as being most distinctly mere continuations of the currency of the Empire. It is only on coins of the lower denominations that we have the distinct names of the Teutonic kings. On the gold coins the monograms of the names sometimes appear in the field, but in all other respects the piece is simply a copy of the current Roman coinage. And the silver and copper are modelled almost as closely upon the Roman types.

Farther away from the ancient centre of government, more characteristic barbarian coinages began to appear. They began in every case with mere imitations of the current coins of the Empire, such as Pl. IV. No. 66, which is simply a Visigothic copy of a coin of Anastasius (cf. No. 65), or No. 59, which is a Frankish imitation of a coin of Mauricius (cf. No. 57). These early types become more and more barbarous, until we get No. 67, the earliest Visigothic coin with the name of the ruler, a coin of Leovigild (A.D. 573—586), obviously imitated from No. 66 or some similar coin. In the same way No. 59, by successive degradations, becomes something like No. 60, a

---

[6] Friedländer, *Münzen der Ostgothen*, and *Num. Chron.*, N.S. xviii, xix., *Coinages of Western Europe from Honorius to Charlemagne* (the present writer).

[7] Friedländer, *Münzen der Vandalen*. This writer makes the coinage begin with Huneric. But this is an error. See *Coinages of Western Europe*, l.c.

Merovingian coin of the north of the Frankish kingdom.[8] Gradually the coinage of each barbaric nation began to take a distinctive character, until it fell into the several classes enumerated above. It will generally be enough to examine the principal types of each class of coins to detect the Roman prototypes from which they have been derived.

The characteristic Merovingian types are as follows :—

Almost all have a bust upon the obverse imitated from the bust on the Roman coins (cf. Pl. IV., Nos. 56, 57, 59, 60, 61).

The reverses have :—

1. A plain cross, or a cross standing upon a ball, often enclosed in a wreath.

2. Another type of the cross is raised upon one or more steps, and has often letters at the sides. This type is known as the Marseilles type. It is copied from the coins of Tiberius and Mauricius, and was introduced into Gaul about A.D. 585.

3. Another form of the cross has a curious anchor-like top, and is hence known as the cross ancrée (No. 61). It is not represented on Roman coins. Sometimes it is so arranged as to have the appearance of a monogram, or of a very degraded head, facing. How far it is an original type I am not able to say.

4. The so-called *ampulla* type shows on the reverse a figure somewhat like a cup. I am disposed to consider it a *re-formed* degradation, either from a facing bust, or from the facing figure of Victory, so common on the Roman coinage of this period.

---

[8] Dorsted, the great emporium for the northern trade. It was situate on the Waal mouth of the Rhine, near where Wijk Te Duerstede now stands.

5. Occasionally we have one or more standing figures on the reverse.

And 6. One remarkable type has on the obverse a facing bust with long hair, like the head of Christ on the later Byzantine coins.

The Lombard coins are divisible into two classes—(1) the Lombard kings of Pavia; and (2) the Dukes of Beneventum and Salerno. The coinages of the two dynasties are wholly distinct.

The characteristic types of the kings of Pavia are two, namely:—

1. *Obv.*—Profile bust of Roman type.

Rev.—An angel (St. Michael) standing to l., holding a staff on the top of which are three balls.[9] (Pl. IV. No. 62 a coin of Cunipert, A.D. 688—700.)

This is undoubtedly derived from the common type, with a standing Victory on the reverse, holding a long cross. (Pl. IV. No. 56.)

2. The second type has on one side a flower, on the other side a cross potent.

It only arose after the influence of the Carling dynasty had become paramount in Western Europe, and is in a great degree an imitation of the Carlovingian coinage.

The coinage of the Lombards of the south—the Dukes of Beneventum, &c.—is of a totally different character from that of the kings of Pavia. It belongs, in fact, to the series of coinages derived from the Byzantine coinage, and as such will be spoken of in its proper place.

---

[9] The three balls are always very distinct upon the top of the staff. This would of course lead a numismatist to identify them as the arms of Lombardy. But *arms* can scarcely be said to belong to this period, and whether these balls are any sort of badge or are there purely by accident I cannot say.

Before speaking of the Visigothic coinage we may briefly notice a small series of coins struck by the Suevi when, driven back by the Visigoths, they were hemmed in within the narrow borders of the Lusitanian province. Hence the coins are called Suevo-Lusitanian. The type of these coins, which have been exclusively found in Portugal, is uniform, and is a rather peculiar adaptation of one of the types of Honorius, having on the obverse a profile bust, and on the reverse a small cross enclosed in a wreath.[10] No. 63 shows the prototype and No. 64 the imitation. There were but four different types in use among the Visigoths of Spain.

1. The type of No. 67 already given, whose origin there is no difficulty in tracing. (Heiss, Monn. des Rois Wisigoths d'Espagne, Pl. I. Nos. 1—4, 6.)

This type belongs only to the earlier years of the Visigothic coinage.

2. Type with similar *obverse*, and for *reverse* a cross haussée upon three steps, as on numerous Byzantine solidi from the time of Mauricius onwards. (Heiss, o. c., Pl. I. Nos. 5, 7, &c.)

A sufficient number of illustrations would show the resemblance of the obverse of this type when first introduced to the preceding obverse type, and its gradual change as we proceed along the line of kings.

3. *Obv.*—Bust facing.

Rev.—Bust facing. (Heiss, o. c., Pl. I. Nos. 8, &c.)

The obverse type here is clearly a rude imitation of the facing bust on the Byzantine coins, and the reverse is a repetition of the obverse.

---

[10] *Rev. Num.*, 1865, p. 235 *seq.*, Pl. IX.

These are the only three types of general use. The coins of Egica and Wittiza (696—700), however, introduce a new type.

4. *Obv.*—Long cross ; at sides two busts counter gardant.
Rev.—Cruciform monogram. (Heiss, o. c., Pl. XI. Nos. 2—9, &c.)

This is the only Visigothic coin which has no certain Byzantine prototype. Of the relationship between this type and some types on other contemporary coins of Western Europe we will speak presently.

It will be seen that besides this lateral (*i.e.* territorial) division between the coinages of different countries, there is also, in almost every series, a vertical line of cleavage, namely, between the coins imitated from the money of the Western Empire and that which is distinctly Byzantine in character. But the true parentage must in every case be assigned to the prototype of the earliest copies. This is why we have classed all the series above enumerated under the head of the descendants of the true Roman coinage. They all sprang up before the Byzantine varieties of coin type had been properly developed. The series of coins which were undoubtedly influenced solely by the Byzantine currency of a later period are classed apart, and will be treated of hereafter. We have now dealt with the most immediate offspring of the Roman coinage. But some of these descendants produced in their turn fresh species of coin, which became in the second degree related to the Roman Imperial coinage. We will next speak of this class, which, spreading out into many ramifications, must, I think, be counted the outgrowth originally of the Merovingian coinage.

First among these subsidiary coinages we come to a series whose origin has somewhat exercised the ingenuity of numismatists, but as yet without any very definite results. I mean the series of earliest English coins, most of them anonymous, which preceded the introduction of the penny into England. The great majority of these pieces are of silver, and it is generally admitted that they are the pieces of which there is occasional mention in the early English laws and literature under the name of *sceattas*. There are some difficulties in the way of reconciling the information which we gather from the Anglo-Saxon laws with the relative weight of the *sceatta* and the *penny*. But still I think we may assume that these small thick pieces were *sceattas*, and may therefore (having in view the immense preponderance of silver) describe the whole class of coins to which they belong as the sceatta class. North of the Humber arose a class of coins similar in general shape and appearance to the sceattas, but with some marked differences of plan, distinguished from them, too, by being nearly always of copper. These pieces are the *stycas*.

The *sceattas*, though not so closely as the Continental coins connected with the Roman currencies, belong to the period of numismatic history which intervened between the fall of Rome and the complete reorganization of the Empire (wherewith went a complete reorganization of the coinage of the West) by Charlemagne. The reorganization of the coinage of Western Europe and the introduction of the new silver denarius on the Continent was almost immediately followed by the introduction of the penny into England. Complicated and difficult to trace as are all the new currencies of Western Europe at this time, our early English coinage is by far the most complicated and most difficult. We will take account of the various influences to which this last was subject, not in the order of their historical sequence but of their potency. As we have already many times insisted, in tracing the descent of a coinage we have to take account of the general character of that coinage as a whole before we examine into the types of individual species. It is this general character which allows us to place all the early electrum staters in one class, and to trace the family likeness between the coinages of Alexander and his successors. Such a general family resemblance is found, not only in all the pennies struck in England after th introduction of the penny, but between these pennies and all the new denarii struck on the Continent from the time of Charlemagne onwards. Such a general family resemblance, despite differences of metal and of type, must be noticed between the later Merovingian coins and the English sceattas. The distance between the two coinages, of which the former is almost wholly in gold and the latter in silver, is bridged over by the discovery of a certain number of gold pieces closely resembling the Merovingian coins, but evidently struck in England. The most remarkable series of this kind was that of the well-known Crondale find, a hoard of 100 gold pieces discovered in the parish of Crondal or Crondale (on Bagshot Heath), Hants, in the year 1828.[11] Among these are some coins which bear the name of a French moneyer, Abbo; and on this account Vicomte Ponton d'Amécourt[12] argues that Abbo must have come

[11] *Num. Chron.* O. S. vol. vi., p. 171.—C. Lefroy and F. Y. Akerman. N. S. vol. x., p. 164.—Sir H. Lefroy. "He [Mr. Akerman] identified several of them as unquestionably belonging to the series of *tiers de sol* or *gold triens* of the French kings of the first race and their moneyers which are occasionally found in England, more especially in those counties which border on the sea-coast opposite France."—Sir H. Lefroy. It must be said, however, that Akerman's attempt at a minute identification of the types strays often very wide of the mark.

[12] *Annuaire de Numismatique*, T. iii., p. 299.

over to England and worked in this country between the years A.D. 593 and 604; and his argument is, to some degree, endorsed by Mr. Kenyon in his *Gold Coins of England*:—"Assuming as an indisputable fact that the greater part of the coins found at Crondale were struck in England, he [Vicomte P. d'Amécourt] concludes that Abbo was one of the Franks who accompanied St. Augustine to England. . . . If this be so—and the ascertained facts certainly seem to make it probable—then this coin, rude as it is, becomes of extreme interest. . . ." [13]

I confess myself unable to follow the reasoning in either case. It is easier for coins to travel than individuals; and the same reasoning which proved that Abbo worked in England might go to show that Philip of Macedon travelled in Gaul and Augustus in Britain. Nor can one see why Abbo, in defiance of Horace, should so completely change his "mind" with his "sky," that the style of the coins made by him in England should be clearly distinguishable from the style of the coins he made while he was in France; and yet, what proof save that of style can there be that the coins were made in this country? If these Crondale coins with the name of Abbo are clearly of a different fabric from the Merovingian pieces,[14] it is more reasonable to imagine that they are simply imitations of the Merovingian money, just as British coins with the name Φιλίππος are imitations of Gaulish coins bearing the same name.

---

[13] *Gold Coins of England*, p. 5.

[14] It is impossible to judge of such a matter from an engraving, and the Crondale coins have not even been photographed. It is many years since they were in my hands, and my attention was not at the time particularly directed to them. Mr. Kenyon had them I think in his hands at the time at which he wrote the passage quoted. His judgment then may be pronounced final.

I take the actual impulse towards a native English coinage to have come from the coasts of France, and the supposition is the more reasonable because the impulse towards a native British coinage came precisely in the same way; and because, before the sceattas or native gold coins began to appear, there was a considerable intercourse between the opposite shores of the British Channel, resulting, as we know, in the marriage of more than one King of Kent with a Merovingian princess, and resulting, in a still more important way, in the introduction of Christianity into the Jutish kingdom. I think, then, we may take these Crondale coins as among the earliest native productions of the English in that way. Many of them have the name of London, which a certain number of the sceattas also bear. London was probably at this time still possessed of a municipal government similar to that which it had enjoyed in the days of the Roman occupation, and was still perhaps more of a British than a Saxon town. In speaking, therefore, of the Crondale coins as among the earliest *English* coins, I use the word English to signify the mixed population at this time under the rule of a variety of Anglian and Saxon kings.

M. Gariel[15] says that before the rise to power of the Carling house, a coinage of Merovingian silver money had begun to replace the coinage in gold especially in the north of France. Very few, indeed, of these silver pieces have been published in French numismatic journals, and

---

[15] *Monnaies royales de France sous la race Carlovingienne*, p. 9. "Plus on se rapproche de la fin de la première dynastie, plus la circulation de l'argent se substitue à celle de l'or. Plusieurs découvertes, faites dans le courant de ces dernières années, le prouvent surabondamment."

I do not know the evidence which M. Gariel had before him when making this statement. Several remarkable finds of coins of the sceatta type in Frisia, made many years ago, are published by M. Dirks, in his pamphlet entitled *Les Anglo-Saxons et leurs petits deniers dits sceattas.*[16] The great majority of the pieces composing the hoards consisted of what we ordinarily call sceattas, and which we believe to have been struck in this country. But a certain number of the coins were of types not found in this country. It is a noticeable fact, moreover, that many of these foreign types seem to have lingered on faintly in the earliest coins issued by the house of Heristal,[17] whose associations, we remember, were all with the very country in which this find was made. The weight of the English silver coins and of the pieces which we may fairly call low Frankish is much the same, varying as much as from 14 to 20 grains in each class, and the pieces were evidently interchangeable.[18] These facts, again, point to the close connection of the English sceattas with the coinage of the Merovingian Franks.

We have thus, I think, ascertained that the true origin of the sceattas as a class lies in the Merovingian money. But there were numerous other influences modifying this initial one, and determining the origin of special types of the sceattas. The first English coinage was not the first money which had been coined in this country; and it is hardly possible but that the sceattas, albeit the money of

---

[16] Published also in the *Revue de la Num. Belge*, 5me Série, T. ii., p. 81.

[17] See *Annuaire de Numismatique*, T. iii., p. 306 *seq.*, *Recherches sur l'origine et la filiation des types des premières monnaies carlovingiennes.* (Vte. P. d'Amécourt.)

[18] A long list of weights is given by Dirks, o. c., p. 70.

a new race, would owe something to the other coinages which had preceded them in this country. These were the British and the Romano-British. The first may be left out of account, it had been so completely superseded by the Roman long before the coming of the Angles and the Saxons. But of the Roman coins—the copper coinage especially—large hoards are being constantly brought to light, showing what immense quantities must have been current in this country during the Roman occupation. Many of these pieces are of exceedingly small size for copper coins—the pieces known as *minimi*. They would be therefore very handy for the use of a people who had advanced far enough in civilisation to require small change. I mean by this a people who had completely laid aside the use of barter. And there can be no doubt that during the Roman rule, the Britons in many parts of the island had advanced to such a point. Now at this very day the Spaniards use small Roman and small Arabic copper coins for their small change. After 1,500 years since the retreat of the Roman legions, these memorials of their days still pass from hand to hand as current coins. And the same is the case with the coins of the Amawí Khalífehs, who have disappeared for 500 years. We have no difficulty, therefore, in believing that the small Roman copper coins remained in use among the more civilised Britons for centuries after the incoming of the Saxons. Roman gold, too, may have remained in use, for the Saxons coined almost exclusively in silver. We have indisputable evidence that many of the sceatta types were copied from one or other of these two classes of Roman coins. Pl. IV., No. 69 is a coin of Maximus struck in London. Readers of Gildas or Bæda will remember how these writers speak of Maximus as being the remote cause of the subjugation of Britain, by reason of his having withdrawn the flower of her youth to fight his battles in Gaul. No. 70 is one of the few Saxon gold coins obviously copied from the Roman type. The same type is also found on the sceattas. There are examples not less certain of the imitation of copper coins. Nos. 71 and 72 are copper coins of Constantine II.; and No. 73 is a specimen of the imitation of the type upon a sceatta. There are numerous other examples not quite so patent of imitations of Roman types on the sceattas.

The variations which take place in the types of the sceattas are suggestive of the changes through which the Gaulish and British coinage passed, beginning first as mere imitations, and then gradually developing a new design out of this imitation—designs, too, of a fanciful rather than a truly artistic or imaginative character. One example is given in the plate of the development of a new design out of the profile taken from the Roman coins. At one time I (following M. Dirks) supposed that the type was developed out of another sceatta type (also of Roman origin), that of the wolf and twins. Now I am convinced that the series is as it is given in the plate.

The accompaniment of these different obverses (Nos. 74—78) by the same or a similar square compartment on the reverse (copied from No. 73), and certain incidental accompaniments of the obverse throughout, as the cross before the face (Nos. 74, 75, 77), the circle before the face, which appears first in No. 76, will, I trust, be enough to convince the reader of this stream of development into the bird-type of No. 78, although it has been necessary to omit a certain number of intermediate types which would have made the process of evolution more apparent. Such instances of the creation of fanciful or even fantastic new types out of old ones, which we find here and in the case of the Gaulish and British series, are on the whole rare in the history of numismatics. Judging from the coins alone we might be inclined to think that it was peculiarly Celtic. But when we look at the history of ornament generally among savage or semi-barbarous nations, we find numerous instances of the same process in far distant quarters of the world. The same element is very markedly present in what is called Scandinavian art, though whether this be not properly speaking Celtic art may be open to question.

It is worth noticing that the coins of the sceatta-type struck with the legend LVNDONIA, and the coins of similar type without that legend, are many of them of almost unmixed copper; very few are of fine silver. These pieces were in use, we may suppose, among a section of the people who had not materially changed their habits since the days of Roman occupation, and who, more than their country neighbours, were still employing for small change the old Roman copper coinage. But the region where the impress of Roman customs might be supposed most strongly stamped was that of the Roman capital, York. Very large finds of Roman coins have been made north of the Humber, as far north as the Roman wall. We may probably account in this way for the prevalence of a copper or very base silver currency north of the Humber. We may take it for a sign of the permanency of Roman influence, at any rate in this matter of a currency. The very earliest Northumbrian *styca* which is known seems to be simply of copper. It is only in its metal that it has any connection with the preceding Roman coinage—its metal, and to some degree its size and shape. But in these latter characteristics it also approaches the sceattas. It has one remarkable element of originality, viz., in the smallness of the type and the importance of the legend. Some one or two of the succeeding Northumbrian kings struck coins which were as often of silver as of copper, and which bear designs closely allied to the designs on the sceattas. Altogether, looking at the Northumbrian coinage from Ecgfrith to Elfwald (670—788), it seems scarcely possible to separate it by a strong line of demarcation from the coinage south of the Humber. But from the reign of Heardwulf (795) onwards, the *stycas* of the north have a character peculiar to themselves. They eschew types, and devote their whole space to the legends. Such a change is of the highest importance. It is analogous to the change which separates the earliest Arab coinage from the Sassanian coinage which preceded it. It is hardly likely that so important an innovation on previous custom should have originated independently within the narrow area of Northumbria; and if, abandoning this country, we turn once more to the coinage of the Continent, we can, I think, detect the cause of this change.

It has been already said that there is a small series of late Merovingian silver coins which form a sort of link between the currencies of the first two dynasties. By the introduction of what was at first known as the *new denarius*, the Austrasian dynasty completely revolutionised the coinages of Western Europe, and the effects of this revolution lasted for at least five centuries. The new denarius is that flat, thin silver piece so wholly different in shape and appearance from any Merovingian coin, so characteristic of the coinage of all the kings of the house of Charlemagne.

Figs. A 1, A 2, B 1, B 2, C 1, C 2, taken from the essay of Vicomte P. d'Amécourt already referred to,[19] show one or two instances in which the earliest Carling pennies

---

[19] *Recherches*, &c., in *Ann. de Num.* iii. 306.

are indebted to the silver currency which preceded them; A 1, B 1, C 1, being the Merovingian silver coins; A 2, B 2, C 2, the Carlovingian. These new denarii begin in the reign of Pepin the Short. They are officially mentioned in a Capitulary of the year 781; and in A.D. 794 we find a decree of Charles the Great making them legally current throughout the Frankish kingdom. Even such

A 1. A 2.

B 1. B 2.

C 1. C 2.

small remnants of a design or *type* as appear on the coins of Pepin and Charles given by Vicomte Ponton d'Amécourt as transition types are absent from the great majority of early Carling coins, which consist simply of a legend without any type (Pl. V. Nos. 79, 80). For a while, then, the use of designs seems to disappear almost as completely from the coinage of Northern Europe (one country being only a partial exception), as it disappears from the Arab coinage when first introduced. These two examples of a people dispensing altogether with designs upon their coins are so striking that we are at once led to consider whether there can have been any connection between the two; whether the type of the Arab coinage can have had any influence in determining the type of the European. Now it is quite possible that such may have been the case. We know that Arab dirhems had by this time obtained a considerable currency in Western Europe. It so happened (though probably only as the result of an accident), that the Amawí, or Abbási *dirhem*, was as nearly as possible the double of the *denarius* or *penny* of Western Europe. The weights of both classes are, indeed, very irregular. But the first range from 40 to 50 grains, and the latter generally from 20 to 24 grains. Both gold and silver Arab coins (*dínárs* and *dirhems*) were occasionally imitated in Western Europe. We have, for instance, the celebrated copy of an Arab dínár, with a mere imitation of the Arabic legend, but with the name of Offa written across the field;[20] which is full of significance for the subject we are discussing. At the latter end of the period with which we are concerned we have a denarius bearing on one side the name and type of Henry II. of Germany, and on the other the type of Hishám II., Khalif of Cordova.[21] The large number of dirhems found in some deposits in England,[22] and a great many more deposits in the Scandinavian countries, are further evidence in point. It seems, then, a not wholly unreasonable supposition that the changes in the disappearance of all design from the

---

[20] Kenyon, *Gold Coins of England.* Frontispiece.

[21] Dannenberg, *Die Deutschen Münzen der Sächs. u. Fränk. Kaiserzeit*, Pl. LIII. No. 1185.

[22] *Coins found at Cuerdale*, by E. Hawkins.

Carling denarii was a change due to some extent to familiarity with the Arabic coinage. The latter pieces, I mean, may have been the first to suggest to Pepin and to Charles the possibility of dispensing with a design upon coins.[23]

The introduction of the new denarius into the Frankish kingdom is, whatever the cause of it, and from whatever point of view we regard it, a change greater than the coinage of Western Europe has since undergone. It makes a complete or almost complete alteration in the metal of the currency, putting silver in the place of the old Merovingian gold currency. It seemed at once to efface all remembrance of the older Roman Empire, for no trace of the type of the Roman coins is to be found on the Carling denarii; and though it was, to a certain extent, modelled upon the Roman weight system in that the Roman pound was still the standard weight, it was adapted to no special modification of that system in use for the Roman monetary system, but was, on the contrary, adapted to tally likewise with a German metric system which had been developed long before. Lastly and not inappropriately, while it seemed to repudiate connection with the old Roman Empire, it reasserted, much more decisively than the Merovingian coinage had done, the authority of the Frankish ruler under whom it was issued. The Merovingian coinage during the latter years had been almost anarchic. A great majority of the pieces issued made no

---

[23] When this paper was read before the Numismatic Society the President, Mr. J. Evans, made a further suggestion relative to the use of Arab coins in the West, that the word sterling (esterling, easterling), for which so many origins have been suggested, may have been derived from the purity of the silver in use for the Arab coins, which were currently known as *easterlings*.

open reference to the king under whom they were struck. The bust which most of them bear may be considered to represent the king, but his name is nowhere inscribed; only the moneyer who struck the coin, and sometimes the mint where he struck it, being given on the coins. In the case of the Carling coinage we have once more the name of the monarch always present; sometimes nothing else but his name appears upon the coins.

This change in the Continental coinage was almost immediately followed by a similar change in England, where the small, thick *sceatta* was exchanged for the penny—a coin much thinner and broader than the *sceatta*, and in every respect of general appearance modelled upon the Carling denarius. There can be little doubt that Offa was the author of the change in England; and we should probably consider as the earliest of his coins those which most nearly resemble some type of Carlovingian coins.[24] The English never dispensed with designs upon their coins, and only partially dispensed with the use of busts modelled upon the bust on Roman coins. The pennies of most of the early reigns may be divided into two classes—those without the bust of the king, and those with it. Offa's coins are peculiar, original, and of great artistic excellence. But those of his successors fall back upon more conventional types, and in these—*i.e.* especially in the bust on the obverse—the influence of the Roman coinage once more becomes apparent.

Even on the coins of Charlemagne there are some exceptions to the general repudiation of Roman types; and in the reign of his successor there was a still further rever-

[24] Such as Nos. 82, 83 of the Plates. Compare the Carlovingian coins, Pl. V. No. 80, and B 2, C 2; also Gariel, o. c., Pl. I. 32; V. 11; IX. 115.

sion towards the use of designs upon the coinage. The Emperor Louis le Débonnaire—Louis the Pious—struck a considerable number of pieces bearing his bust. He returned, moreover—we may note this in passing—in some degree to the use of gold coins, which had been completely abandoned by his predecessor. Neither of these changes was permanent. A gold coinage was not revived in Western Europe until another three or four centuries had passed.[25]

The bust, again, which appears very sparsely on the coins of Charlemagne, and much more frequently on those of Louis, was once more practically abandoned. It was revived somewhat a century later by Louis IV. d'Outremer (936—954). As we shall see anon, this bust had a considerable influence on the formation of later coin-types.

Another type largely used upon the coins of Louis the Pious, though it seems to have been invented by Charlemagne,[26] was the *Temple* or *Christiana Religio* type. It consisted of the front of a temple or basilica, with the words 'Xristiana Religio' written round it.[27] It was

[25] The revival of a gold currency may be dated from the first issue of gold ducats, by princes of Apulia, in the middle of the twelfth century. But the beginning of an extensive gold coinage dates from the coinage of the gold florin, A.D. 1257.

[26] Gariel, Pt. II., Pl. XII. 169—170.

[27] There may possibly be two reverse types originally different which produced the series of imitations spoken of here as the *temple* type. (See Pl. V. 84, 85). They are taken to be so by Lelewel, *Num. du Moyen Age*, Atlas Pl. VIII. He speaks of the "portail" and the temple types. Cf. Gariel, *Découverte de Veuillin*, Pt. I. Pl. III., No. 5; *Découverte de la Haye*, Pl. VI. 15—16; Pt. II. Pl. V. 9; XV. 27—32; XVIII. 98, 119; XIX. 123, 128, 133—5, and Pt. I. Pl. VI. 7—14, 17; Pt. II. Pl. XII. 169—170; XVII. 81, 82; XX. 4, 6—8, 13. In Pl. XXI. the two types seem to approach nearer and nearer, and I doubt if after this time (*temp.* Charles the Bald) a distinction can be perceived between them.

originally an Italian type, and there seems no reason to doubt that the basilica represented is the basilica of St. Peter at Rome. For a long time the *temple* type was most in use on the Italian coinage of successive emperors, so that those emperors or kings of the Carling race who had the closest connection with Italy are they on whose coins this type is most frequent. Lothar, for instance, the successor of Louis the Pious, and his son, Lothar II., both used the type with great frequency, and it was probably through the latter that it became firmly established as a Lotharingian type. Hence it spread farther into Germany, and, as we shall see presently, it became the parent of a vast number of types of the cities and feudatories of the Empire. A specimen of this temple type is given in Pl. V. No. 84.

Another type of great future importance was that of the 'Karolus' monogram. It was introduced and not infrequently used by Charles the Great.[28] But it was Charlemagne's grandson, Charles the Bald, who gave it its widest circulation. It is specially ordained in one of his decrees, in the Edict of Pitres (864), where the exact description of the coinage which he established is given in the following words—"Ut in denariis novæ [monetae] nostræ ex unâ parte nomen nostrum habeatur in gyro, et in medio nostri nominis monogramma, ex altera vero parte nomen civitatis et in medio crux habeatur" (c. xi.) Or, in modern numismatic language:—

> *Obv.*—In centre within a circle the monogram K-$\underset{L}{\overset{R}{\Diamond}}$-S (Karolus) and around outside circle CARLUS REX.
>
> *Rev.*—In centre within circle, cross pattée; around, name of city, &c. (Gariel, o. c., Pl. XII. 186, and comp. Pl. V. No. 86).

---

[28] Gariel, Pt. II., Charlemagne, Pl. XII., XIII., Nos. 181—216.

This type had a great influence upon the future of the coinages of Northern Europe. The use of monograms upon coins had always been a rather specially favourite device of the Teutonic nations. Small monograms appear upon the coins of the Ostrogoths and Vandals, and are not infrequent on those of the Merovingian kings. Pepin and Charlemagne first introduced much larger monograms, filling up frequently the whole face of the coin; and the influence of the Frankish coinage caused the imitations of these devices on, *e.g.*, the coins of the Visigoths of Spain and of the Dukes of Beneventum in South Italy. But this 'Karolus' monogram has a peculiar compactness and neatness of execution which was then new upon coins, but which from that time forward became common. Among the numerous devices formed upon the same pattern, one introduced by Odo or Eudes, the first king of the Capet house, deserves notice. It is not so much a monogram as a peculiar arrangement of the letters ODO, combined with a cross,[29] or sometimes into the monogram of RX (for Rex). The cross became so common—so nearly universal on the one side or other of the early French Baronial coinage, that it is only the Karolus monogram which affords us a distinctive type. We shall distinguish this type, therefore, as the *Karolus monogram* type. We shall speak of the *Odo monogram* when we refer to the special variety introduced by Odo. The three essentially distinct types—the *bust*, the *temple*, and the *monogram*, will be found to have produced the great majority of coin types on the later feudal coinage of France and Germany. We will first examine two of the most important modifications of the *bust* and *temple* types, and then proceed to a general

---

[29] Gariel, o. c., Pt. II., Pl. XLVII. 40.

classification of the later French currency (such of it as is certainly imitated) under the types from which it was derived.

D 1. D 2. D 3. D 4. D 5. D 6.

Fig. D 1 is a coin of Chinon, having on the obverse a bust of the same type as that of Louis d'Outremer. It was apparently struck about the middle of the tenth century. At this time Chinon had come into the possession of Thibault the Trickster, who was likewise Duke of Chartros. Through successive degradations, as given in Figs. D 2, D 3, D 4, D 5, D 6, the Chinon coin reaches the strange form known as the Chartres type; and this type, unintelligible as it is, became comparatively stereotyped, and had a very wide circulation and a wide influence. To see how wide, we must study the coinage of Chartres, Romorantin,

Château du Loir, Perche, &c., or the engravings of these coins in the works of the Baronial coins of France by Duby or Poey d'Avant. It is difficult to believe that such a sudden degradation of a type resulting in the stereotyping of one meaningless form of it was simply the result of the barbarism of the people who copied and used the coin. Besides, the degradation does not seem to me to be of the kind which we are accustomed to in simply barbarous imitations. Let us compare it, for example, with any of the examples of the most barbarous imitations cited in the first part of this essay—Himyarite imitations of Attic tetradrachms, British copies of Macedonian staters, or what not—and we must, I think, see that it differs in character wholly from these. The reason is, I think, that we trace here the influence of an effort at assimilation of this Chartres coinage to the monogram coinages—the types founded on the Karolus monogram—which, when it began to spring up, were the prevailing types in France.

I believe the same sort of cross influences are to be traced in the formation of the well-known *Tours* type, which became, in later times, one of the most characteristic types of the regal coinage. The Tours type was obviously a development from the *Temple* type. Figs. E 1, E 2, E 3, E 4, show the process of its evolution; and the more detailed series given in the plates of Poey d'Avant's *Monnaies féodales de France* serve more fully to convince us of that. But it is, I think, like the Chartres type, a degradation under the influence of the *Karolus-monogram* type. It is worth noticing how, with the revival of trade, this type, like many others more or less accidentally produced, becomes stereotyped. (Comp. Pl. V., No. 87, coin of Louis IX.)

It would take far too long were we to examine the descent of the whole of the Baronial coinage in the same detail that we have that of these two important series of Touraine and Chartres. But the reader may do this for himself in the plates of the excellent book to which I have already referred, the *Monnaies féodales de France*, by Poey d'Avant. And in order to assist his search, we will range the whole series of coin-imitations into three classes, those which can be traced back ultimately—(1) to the type of the *bust* of Louis I., imitated by Louis IV.; (2) to the *temple* type; and (3) to the *Karolus* or monogram type. A sub-class of the latter is formed by those which follow the "Odo" variety of monogram. The references are to the plates in Poey d'Avant. The numbering of the plates is continuous throughout the three volumes.

1.—Bust.

Brittany (Pl. VIII.—X).

Ponthièvre (Pl. XXVII). A very curious degradation of the profile bust.

Blois, Chartres, &c. (Pl. XXXII.—XL. 8).

Provence (Pl. CVI.).

Sens (Pl. CXXXVII. 6—9). I believe this type, called a *comb*, to have been originally degraded from a profile bust. Comp. sceattas, Pl. IV. 76—78. Should my supposition be correct it would quite change the order in which the pieces are arranged by Poey d'Avant. For the least like a comb would probably be the earliest as most near to the original bust.

2.—Temple.

Normandy (Pl. III.—VI.). Special form of temple type peculiar (almost) to this district.
Touraine (Pl. XXXI. 6—18). Development of the Tours type already spoken of.
Toulouse (Pl. LXXIX.—LXXXI.) has some types derived from the Tours type.
Lyons, Abps. of, Burgundian type (Pl. CXII. 12—21). Notice especially No. 21.
Sens, Cts. of (Pl. CXXXVI. 13, 16, 17).
Quentovic (Pl. CLIII., 5—8.—CLIV. 9). Some degradations of *temple* type.
Montreuil (Pl. CLV. 1—11).

3a.—Karolus Monogram (Pitres).

Duché de France (Pl. I. II. 1—21). Many of these developments of the *monogram* type are modified by the influence of the *temple* type.
Brittany (Pl. VIII.—X.). Most of these modifications are peculiar to Brittany.
Anjou (Pl. XXVIII.—XXIX. 10). Successive degradations of this type till it takes the form of a key or keys.
Maine (Pl. XXIX. 14—XXX. 18). The persistent series of the Counts of Maine begins with the coins having the monogram of Herbert I. (1015—1036). But this is imitated from the *Karolus* monogram. The monogram finally turns into a crown.
Nevers (Pl. XLVI. 6—21).
Poitou (Pl. LII.—LV.). Numerous, but not important modifications of the Karolus monogram, and of the cross of the Pitres type.
La Marche (Pl. LVI—LVII.). Interesting modifications of same type.
Aquitaine (Pl. LIX. 1—15). The early coins of Aquitaine were derived directly from the Pitres type.
Toulouse (Pl. LXXIX. 9—LXXXI. 12). Modifications of both *Karolus* and *Tours* types.
Narbonne (Pl. LXXXII.). Modifications both directly from *Karolus* monogram, and indirectly from *Odo* monogram.
Béziers (Pl. LXXXIV. 15—LXXXV. 1—12).
Provence (Pl. CV. 15—24).
Lyons, Cts. of (Pl. CXIII. 4—9).

Chalons (Pl. CXXIX. 15—27).
Champagne (Pl. CXXXV. 5, &c.).
Champagne Troyes (Pl. CXXXVII. 11—18.—XXXVIII.).
Quentovic (Pl. CLIII.—CLIV.). Degradations of both *temple* and *Karolus* types.
Artois (Pl. CLVII. 1—7).

3b.—Odo Monogram.

Narbonne (Pl. LXXXII.).
Carcassonne (Pl. LXXXIII. 4—18).

In France proper, then, that is to say, in all the region west of Lotharingia, the *monogram* type had a greater influence in the formation of the later coinage than any other of the Carling coin types. The Tours type, indeed, came eventually to occupy a very conspicuous place in the French coinage, from its survival in the royal currency after the greater number of the baronial currencies had disappeared. In this way the importance of the *temple* type was vindicated. But this was in some sense an accidental circumstance. It does not interfere with the fact that the number of separate types of feudal coins which grew out of the *monogram* type was, in France proper, very much greater than the types which grew out of the *temple* type or out of the *bust* type.

In Lorraine and in Germany, as we shall see, the state of things was entirely reversed. There is altogether a greater variety in German coins than there is in the French. Some of the types seem decidedly original; some, as we shall see presently, are certainly copied from the types on the Byzantine coins. There remain, however, a very large number (a great majority, in fact) of the actual pieces which are derived from the Carling types.

In Dannenberg's monumental work, *Die Deutschen Münzen der Sächsischen u. Fränkischen Kaiserzeit*, we have the fullest list of German coins subsequent to the Carling era. And among the different series there represented we separate those under the heads of the Carling types from which they are derived. The numbers in this list, except when placed within brackets, refer to the *plates* of Dannenberg. The numbers in brackets are those of individual coins. The Carling types which we find to have influenced the development of the later German coinage are—

1. The old *Charlemagne* type, by which the legend on one side or the other fills up the whole face of the coin (Pl. V. No. 80 *obv.*).
2. The *temple* type.
3. The *monogram* type.

And the following is the list of the derived coinages, with the references to Dannenberg:[30]—

CHARLEMAGNE TYPE.

Cologne, 14—15, and the following allied or derived series.
Remagen, 18.
Paderborn, 32.
Soest, 32.
Breisach (905*b*).

TEMPLE TYPE.

Metz, 1.
Toul (?), 4.
Verdun, 5, with numerous new forms also.
Lower Lorraine, 6.
Antwerp, 6. Compare with these the coins of Normandy.
Flanders, 7.
Xanten, 13. Merely a reminiscence of the temple.
Cologne, 15 (352), 16, 17 with changed forms (cf. 389, 391, &c.).
Andernach, 19.
Trèves, 20.
Deventer, 24 (569).
Magdeburg, 28. With interesting changes.

---

[30] Cf. also No. 88 of Pl. V., which is a coin of Otho III. (996—1002), a late and degraded form of the *temple* type.

Mainz, 34. With developed types.
Speier, 36.
Worms, 36, 37.
Würzburg, 37.
Erfurt, 38.
Strassburg, 40.
Basle (972).
Chur (976).
Augsburg, 44, 45.
Regensburg, 46, 47, 48.
Cham, 49.
Eichstädt, 49.
Nabburg, 49.
Neuburg, 50.
Salzburg, 50.

MONOGRAM TYPE.

Some of the coinages of Otho I. and Otho III. are remotely derived from the other 'Odo' monogram.

Würzburg, 38.
Zürich, 43.
(With Otto monogram.)
Würzburg, 37.

The influence of the Carling coinage was paramount north of the Alps. But imperial mints existed in many of the larger cities of Italy, especially in Northern Italy, as in Venice, Milan, Pavia, and Lucca. And the early coinages of these cities follow generally the imperial types. In other cases, as, for instance, that of Rome, the coinage came almost immediately under the influence of the Carling coinage. The earliest Papal coin is a denarius of Adrian I., Byzantine in type, and in fact closely resembling the money of the Dukes of Beneventum. But the denarii of his successor, Leo III. (the same who placed the imperial diadem upon the head of Charles the Great) are evidently of the Frankish type; and such, with certain side influences, the denarii of the Popes continued to be for about a century. After that the coinage of Italy began to pass over to the Byzantine influence.

We have to notice one or two smaller series of coins, and then we have come to the end of those which can fairly be counted the offspring of the Carlovingian denarius. We have seen that the whole series of English pennies owes its origin to this Carling coin; so, therefore, in a remoter degree, do the coinages which sprang from the English penny. These may be enumerated in the order in which they arise.

1. The so-called Hiberno-Danish coins struck by the Danish (or, perhaps, rather, Norse) kings in Ireland. It is now an acknowledged fact, thanks to the labours of Dr. Aquilla Smith, that this Hiberno-Danish coinage was derived from the coinage of Æthelred II. Pl. V., No. 89, is a coin of Æthelred II.; No. 90 is a coin of Sihtric III., King of Dublin.

2. The Scandinavian coins. The coinage of Denmark itself was in this manner copied directly from the English coinage of about the same period. Svend Forkbeard was the first Danish king who struck coins. These and those of his successors, Cnut the Great and Harthacnut (Kings of Denmark and England), are all modelled closely upon the English type. No. 91 is a coin of Harthacnut. With the advent of the Ynglinger line there comes a change. Henceforward the types are more varied, and their origin is more difficult to trace. But it is certain that some of these are copied from the type of Byzantine coins.[31]

The earliest coins of Norway and Sweden follow English and Danish types.[32]

---

[31] C. J. Thomsen, *Cat.*, *Les Monn. du Moyen-Age.* T. iii., Pl. IX., X.

[32] C. I. Schive, *Norges Mynter i Middelalderen.* Tab. 1.

3. The Scottish coinage, which begins at a much later period—the reign of David I. (A.D. 1124-1153)—must be reckoned as the third important series which sprang out of the English. For many reigns it imitated closely the contemporary English coins.

We have now come to the end (1) of those coinages which were founded directly upon the Roman coinages; (2) of that vast series of coinages which was founded on the Carlovingian *denarius novus*, which, in its turn, was a partial descendant of one of the classes of coins in the first category. (3) It is finally our business to speak of the currencies which owed their origin to the Byzantine coinage.

The Byzantine coinage is, of course, a derivative of the Roman. In fact, the process of its separate evolution is so gradual that it is very difficult to say at what point it begins to have a distinct character. Perhaps the point of divergence may be best placed at the accession of Justinian the Great.

In the reign preceding Justinian, the bust of the emperor is generally in profile; it is very rarely quite full-face to the front. A not unfrequent attitude of it is turned three-quarters towards the spectator. In this last case it is generally a helmeted bust, and the spear is held behind the head. The profile bust is most frequently diademed, but the diadem is a simple one, more like the old Greek *diadema* or the Roman fillet than a crown. Such is the coinage previous to Justinian the Great. But henceforward the emperor's bust is frequently represented turned full to the front; it is adorned with a heavy jewelled diadem almost like an imperial crown, and the figure holds an orb surmounted by a cross; occasionally in addition, it holds the labarum or a long cross. Then, as we might expect, the more we advance into Christian times the more prominent becomes the position of the cross. In the later Roman or earlier Byzantine coins the most common type is, on the reverse of the coins, that of a Victory, either facing or in profile, and holding either a wreath or a long cross. I call the figure a Victory because its descent from the Victory of heathen times is uninterrupted; but nevertheless it is likely enough that to the Christian population among whom the coin was current its figure passed for an angel. The smaller coins (*trientes*) in Christian times begin sometimes to have simply a cross (sometimes it rests upon a ball) enclosed within a wreath. Later on, the cross often appears alone on both *solidi* and *trientes*. It is, too, from the time of Tiberius II. (574—582) often potent, *i.e.* having its limbs terminated by cross-bars in the fashion of a crutch, and *haussée* (raised) upon three (or fewer) steps. (Cf., Pl. V., Nos. 92, 93, Constantine III.) After this, standing figures of the emperor—of two or more emperors, emperor and empress, &c.—become pretty frequent. These figures often stand on either side of a cross, which sometimes both are holding. The bust of Christ appears upon coins first in the reign of Justinian II., Rhinotmetus (705—712), and in a somewhat changed form it continues to appear until the end of the Byzantine coinage. A full-length figure of Christ enthroned comes in about the middle of the ninth century. The figure generally bears the Gospels in one hand, and sometimes gives the benediction with the other. This seated figure of Christ was one of the most prolific sources of later coin designs. We have, too, a standing figure of Christ, the seated or standing figure of the Virgin, or of some saint, &c.

The distinctly Byzantine types, then, may be enumerated as follows:—

1. Full-face bust of emperor in peculiar square diadem holding an orb, or two emperors seated side by side.
2. Similar standing figure of the emperor, or standing figures of two emperors, cross or labarum between them. (Pl. VI. No. 96).
3. Various forms of cross, the most characteristic being the cross potent, and raised upon steps.
4. Bust of Christ nimbate.
5. Seated nimbate figure of Christ facing, holding Gospels. (Pl. VI. Nos. 96, 97.)
6. Bust or seated figure of Virgin showing in her bosom the nimbate head of the infant Saviour.
7. Christ crowning the emperor, both standing at full length.
8. Virgin crowning the emperor, both standing at full length. (Pl. VI. 97.)
9. Standing figure of the Virgin alone, or of some saint.

The Byzantine coinage gradually spread its influence to Italy, and left it as a legacy to those States which were carved out of the ruins of the Byzantine Empire in Europe. It is enough if we notice here in a summary way the principal series which were derived from it.

The Dukes of Beneventum and Salerno. These Lombards of the south had a coinage quite different from that of the kings of Northern Lombardy. It was modelled directly upon the contemporary Byzantine coinage, as the figures (Nos. 92, 93, Constantine III. and 94, Romvald II., Duke of Beneventum, 707—733) sufficiently show.

So far as a Christian coinage continued in Sicily, this must be reckoned essentially Byzantine in form. The coinage of the Norman dukes of Apulia, Amalfi, Salerno, &c., is chiefly represented by pieces in copper, modelled upon the large copper Byzantine. The same kind of coinage is found among the Crusaders; and, as we have said above, the large copper coinage of the Urtukís and the Bení Zengí Atábegs must be likewise reckoned in some sense the offspring of the Byzantine coinage. As we travel northwards in Italy, we see each State, as it threw off the yoke of the Empire, turning more and more towards the East for the pattern of its coinage. This movement is partly political (*z*), but it is in a great degree likewise a commercial movement. For with the rise of the Carling house, and the spread of the new Carling denarius, gold coins almost ceased to be coined in Western Europe. The result was that the gold currency was supplied from the East in the form of the Byzantine solidi (*solidi Byzantini*), or, as they came to be called, bésants, bezants. Italy, when it began to grow in wealth, felt a much greater need for these gold coins than the countries of the north; and it was natural that the native Italian coinage should tend more and more to model itself upon that of Constantinople. Besides, there was of course a constant and active trade between Italy and the Eastern Empire; and the same influences which brought about the dawn of Italian art were sufficient to reform the Italian coinage.

Thus, in the very earliest Papal coins, we see some influence of Byzantine coin types running alongside of the influence of the Carling denarii (Pl. V., No. 95, Pope Leo III.). When, one by one, the great Italian cities threw off the yoke or freed themselves from the influence of the Western Empire, they adopted new types copied more or less closely from the coinage of Byzantium. Perhaps the most remarkable instance of this change is the coinage of Venice. Up to the time of Enrico Dandolo (1192—1205), Venice struck simply as one of the imperial mints in Italy. But with the accession of this Doge, the coinage was completely transformed into the type given in

Plate VI., No. 98. There is no difficulty in seeing how closely this type is imitated from types of Byzantine gold coins. Compare No. 98, for instance, with the Byzantine coins Nos. 96, 97.

This is the type of the silver ducat. The gold ducat, or sequin, which was not introduced till A.D. 1140, has a somewhat different design, more original than that of the silver coin, but still with a pretty close general resemblance to the Byzantine coinage (Pl. VI., No. 99). On one side is Christ standing within a nimbus of stars; on the other the Doge kneeling, and receiving the gonfalone from St. Mark. Both types became stereotyped under the influence of the commercial activity of Venice; in fact, under the very same influence which stereotyped the coinage of Athens long before. It was not only the Venetian trade, but the fact that that trade lay largely in the East and among barbarous peoples, that kept the coinage so absolutely unchanged. The figure on Pl. VI., No. 100, is a rude copy of a modern Venetian sequin, made, I believe, in Northern Africa. We can trace what was the exact prototype of the African imitation. It is a sequin of Aloysio Mocenigo II. (1700—1709), No. 99. As we have already said, this is perhaps the supreme instance of the barbarous copy of a type, and the neglect of all that gives the type a value, that is to say, the purity of metal and justness of weight of which the type is supposed to be guarantee (see Pt. I. p. 10). What is the exact history of the imitation of this type in Northern Africa, whence these pieces seem always to come, I cannot say, but we may suppose it a reminiscence of a time when the Venetian ducat formed one of the most universal currencies of the Mediterranean. Genoa was another great trading city which had an almost stereotyped coinage. It claimed to have received the right of coinage from Conrad III., and for centuries after the death of this emperor his name still continued to figure on the coins; the type, too—on one side the gateway or doorway (janua), which were the arms of the town, on the other, a plain cross pattée, very much of the Pitres type—remained almost wholly unchanged. Other towns—as Milan and Pavia—when they erected themselves into republics, struck coins more or less of Byzantine types. They showed on one side a seated figure, copied—like the seated Christ on the silver coins of Venice—from the seated figure of Christ on the Byzantine solidi. Each city placed upon the throne the figure of its own saint—St. Ambrose for Milan (Pl. VI. No. 102), St. Sirus for Pavia, &c.

On the whole, it would seem that there were two routes by which the coinage of the Eastern Empire spread its influence westward. By sea it reached Sicily and the South of Italy; and as the Arabic coinage disappeared from the former place, a coinage modelled on the Byzantine coinage took its place. By the land route it passed through Aquileia and Venice into the northern cities of Italy. Hence it is that in the central cities of Italy—in Florence, for instance, and Rome—the Byzantine influence is weakest. The coinage of Florence can scarcely be referred to a Byzantine origin. Still, the figure of St. John the Baptist on the silver money (the earliest coinage) was probably suggested by the Byzantine coin-types of a similar kind (Pl. VI. No. 108).

The gold coinage of Florence—the famous *fiorino d'oro* (No. 109)—is of a more or less original type. But it, in its turn, had an enormous influence on the currency of Europe towards the end of the Middle Ages. Almost all the nations of Europe began their gold coinage with imitations of the *fiorino d'oro.* It is interesting, too, to see how this piece, under the influence of commercial necessity, became stereotyped, much as did the Venetian ducat or sequin. Under commercial influences indeed the coinage always has a tendency to become stereotyped.

Passing eastward, it is natural to find the Byzantine influence still stronger. We come first to the coinage of the Patriarchs of Aquileia, of which No. 104 is an example. It is a coin of Bertoldo, Duke of Meran and Patriarch of Aquileia (1218—1225). The likeness between this and the coinages of Leo VI. and Constantine X. (No. 96) is easily seen. Other pieces show the Patriarch and St. Gregory standing on opposite sides of a long cross, much in the fashion of No. 98 and the Venetian coin from which it is copied. A third type shows the Saint enthroned, as on the coins of Milan and Pavia. Farther east we come to the kingdom of Servia, which, as we know, threw off the yoke of the Byzantine Empire in the middle of the twelfth century. No. 101 is a typical Servian coin It is a piece of Stephan (III.) Orosius (1240—1272).

And we must not, in this connection, fail to notice that very extraordinary find of old Russian coins discovered in Nishin (Nejin), in the Government of Tchernigov, and described by Count Stroganoff and by Count Tolstoy in the pages of the *Zeitschrift für Numismatik.*[33] These pieces are earlier than any other known Russian coinage. It, to my thinking, is not less certain that, as Count Tolstoy has argued, their types are derived from the

[33] Vol. x. pp. 112, 177.

coinage of the Eastern Empire. Two specimens are here given (Figs. F 1, F 2).

F 1. F 2.

North of the Alps, the paramount influence is always traceable back to the Carling denarius. But in Germany, especially alongside of the types derived from this source, such as those which were enumerated just now, there are a considerable number of other types, either quite original, or derived from some other quarter. Some of these types are undoubtedly Byzantine. Such, I believe, is the head of the Virgin (Dannenberg, o. c., No. 716), which belongs to the middle of the eleventh century. Such is undoubtedly the head of the Virgin, with hands upraised, in D. 837—8 and 840, in date *circ.* A.D. 1060—1067 (comp. Pl. VI., No. 103), and D. 1202, an uncertain imperial coin of Henry III. (1039—1056). Such, once more, is the coin of Burkhard II., Duke of Swabia (954—973), showing the figure of Christ enthroned, with the legend IHS XPC REX (D. 901), just as in the Byzantine coins. Still more unmistakeable is the head of Christ among the uncertain German denarii in D. 1187—9, 1242. It is, as Dannenberg says, copied from the coins of Theophilus Michael. Such is possibly the hand in benediction (D. 100, date 990—1024, and 105, date 1039—1046).

We see that the Byzantine influence can be traced in Germany at a sufficiently early date. Besides these certain imitations, I am disposed to see some trace of the same influence in many types which one would, at first sight, be disposed to think were original and peculiar to Germany, such as the following:—

1. The full-faced bust of the emperor, wearing a square diadem or crown, as in our coins of Henry I. The type on our coinage is almost certainly not original. We do, indeed, get a profile bust with not dissimilar crown on the coins of Edward the Confessor and Harold. But we have earlier examples of it on the coinage of the German, to which this elaborate crown is much more appropriate than it is to our kings. Nevertheless, then, I do not think it is wholly original, but at least suggested by the much anterior bust similar in type on the Byzantine coins. (Comp. Pl. V. Nos. 92, 93, but for a much better example, Sabatier, I., Pl. XXVIII. No. 7, Heraclius I.) The number of coins with the facing bust given by Dannenberg is very considerable (cf. Pl. VI. No. 105), but the following may be selected from among the earlier forms of it as most nearly resembling the Byzantine type just referred to, D. 34, 316, 539 (Utrecht), 578 (Thiel), 666, 788. The last (a coin of Mainz) is especially noticeable. One hand evidently once held the cross-bearing orb, as the emperor does on the Byzantine coins, but in the German denarius the type is so far degraded that only the traces of the orb and cross remain. This is strong argument that the type is a copy of some other previous type. But it is earlier than any of the other German denarii cited, being a coin of Henry the Lame (1002—1024). The inference that a Byzantine coin was the prototype of this one, and hence of all the other specimens, is consequently very strong.

2. Another very frequent type on the Imperial series is

the bust or half-figure facing, and holding a book. In addition, it also frequently holds a crozier or pastoral staff (cf. D. 203—4, 207—9, 277, 297, 389, 396—9, 401, 405—7, 410, 412, 416—20, 422, 424, 426, 455—7, 531—7, 551, 631, 820). This may be a purely original type. But it may also be derived from the not dissimilar figure of Christ on the Byzantine coins.

3. Two heads facing, and placed side by side (cf. D. 526—530, 532—4, 634, 649, 667—670, 674, 676, 678, 680, 682—3, 691, 693—7, 700). It need not be said that similar heads or figures are common on Byzantine coins long before they were ever made in Germany.

It must be noticed incidentally how many of the English types must have been suggested by the types of these German denarii.

The bowl-type of German coins, which seems to come in with the house of Saxony, I take to be also a sign of Byzantine influence; and still stronger evidences are to be found in the large bracteates which come in with the Swabian house.

Finally, it is noticeable how largely Byzantine types were copied on the Danish coins after the intrusion of the Ynglinger line. But the fashion is continued by Svend Estrithsen. No. 106 is a coin of Magnus the Good (1042—1047), No. 107 of Svend Estrithsen (1047—1076). The reverse of both, it is curious to notice, is of the old English type.

These investigations bring us down till near the end of the thirteenth century for the coinage of all Europe. After this time the types become so numerous and complicated that only by a very minute examination would it be possible to trace each one back to the parent form. We will therefore bring our inquiry to a close by simply enumerating one or two prominent instances of the copying of coin types of one country by its neighbours.

1. The most important of these is the copying of the florin. The florin of Florence (the *fiorino d'oro*) was first coined in the year 1252. It rapidly spread over most of the countries of Europe, which till then had been generally contented with the bezants as substitutes for a native gold currency. Imitations of the *fiorino d'oro* were made in almost every kingdom in Europe, as follows:—

Italy. Montferrat, Savoy, Savona.

Spain. Aragon (Peter IV., John I., Martin).

France. Aquitaine (Edward III. of England); Arles; Avignon (Pope John XXII.); Bar (Robert, Duke, 1355—1411); Béarn (Gaston de Foix); Burgundy (Odo IV., Philip the Bold ?); Cambray; Dauphiny (Guigues VIII., Humbert II., Charles V., King of France); Lorraine (John I.); Montélimart (Gaucher ?); Orange (Raymond III., Bertram); Provence (Johanna and Louis); St. Paul-trois-Châteaux (Bp. John I.).

Netherlands. Brabant (John III.); Flanders (Louis I.); Gelderland (Reynold II.); Hennegau (William II., Margaret, wife of Emp. Louis IV.); Horn (Dirk-Loef); Cts. of Looz (Dietrich, Godfrey II.); Luxemburg (Wenceslas I.); Valkenberg-Fauquemont (Reynold).

Germany. Cleves (John); Jülich (William I.); Heinsberg (Godfrey III.); Essen (Abbess Elizabeth; this, says Herr Dannenberg, is the last of these pieces struck in Germany); Cologne (Abp. William of Gennep, Adolf II., Ct. of Mark, Abp. Engelbert III.); Trèves (Boemund II., Cuno V.); Mainz (Gerlach, Ct. of Nassau, 1346); Nassau (Ct. Ruprecht); Eppstein (Eberhard I.); Rhinish Palatinate (Rupert I.); Bamberg (Bp. Leopold III.).

Austria. (Albert II., Rudolf IV.); Goerz (Albert IV.); Liegnitz (Wenceslas I.); Münsterberg (Boleslaus II.); Schweidnitz (Boleslaus II.); Bohemia (John); Lübeck.

Hungary. Charles I. and Louis I.

Achaia. Prince Robert II.[34]

---

[34] The above list is taken from a paper by Herr H. Dannenberg in the *Numismatische Zeitschrift* for 1880.

Almost all of these coins belong to the fourteenth century, which therefore, we may suppose, was the time, or immediately subsequent to the time, at which the *fiorino d'oro* had its widest circulation. The coin of the Abbess Elizabeth of Essen, referred to above, may have been struck in the fifteenth century.

2. The English pennies of Edward I., Edward II., and Edward III. were extensively imitated in the Low Countries, *i.e.* by the following princes and states:—Counts of Flanders, Hainault, and Namur; Dukes of Brabant and of Limburg; Bishops of Liège; Lords of Héristal and of Vorst; Counts of Looz and Chiny; Lords of Rummen, of Bunde, and of Agimont; Counts of Luxemburg; Dukes of Lorraine; Counts of Bar; Bishops of Toul and Cambray; Counts of St. Pol, of Porcien, of Ligny, of Rethel, and of Sancerre; and the Dukes of Aquitaine.[35]

3. The English gold coins were many of them imitated from or suggested by the French gold coinage. They, in their turn, were extensively imitated by some of the princes and states of the Low Countries. The chief coins copied in the Low Countries were the nobles of Edward IV. (Brabant and Limburg, Holland, Gelderland), and the angels of Edward IV. and his successors (Brabant and Limburg, Battenburg, Holland).[36]

---

[35] J. Chautard, *Imitations des Monnaies au type Esterlin*, passim.

[36] V. der Chijs, *Munten der Nederl.*, vol. ii., Pl. III., XVII.; vol. iii., Pl. IX. Id. *Munten der voormalige Graafsch. Holl. en Zeel.*, Pl. XL.

DESCRIPTION OF THE COINS ENGRAVED, PARTS I. AND II., PLATES I.—VI.[37]

Nos. 1—55 comprise coinages derived from the Greek coinage (the Greek Family).

1. Electrum stater. This piece adequately represents the earliest class of coins in Lydia, struck early in the seventh century B.C. Whether the actual specimen given, which bears the name of "Phanes," is of such an early date must be a matter of dispute. It has been assigned to Phanes of Halicarnassus.
2. *Persia.* Gold daric. A direct descendant of the electrum staters. First coined B.C. 516. Continued unchanged until after the time of Alexander the Great.
3. *Ægina.* Earliest silver coinage. First half of seventh century B.C. Earliest coinage of European Greece, and likewise a descendant of the electrum coinage.
4. *Athens.* Earliest silver coins. Struck soon after B.C. 590. Derived from coinage of Ægina.

5, 6. *Yemen* (*S. Arabia*). Barbarous copies of the Athenian coinage.

7. *Corinth.* Earliest coinage. Middle of the seventh century.
8. *Italy.* Metapontum. Early flat coinage of Italy derived from Corinthian coinage. Comp. Nos. 7 and 10.
9. *Sicily.* Selinus. Earliest Sicilian coinage. Derived directly from Corinthian (?). Comp. incuse reverses of Nos. 7 and 9.
10. *Corinth.* *Circa* B.C. 600. First modification of incuse anvil-marks into pattern.
11. *Sicily.* Syracuse. Æ. Later Sicilian coinage.
12. *Carthage.* Æ. Phœnician imitation of Syracusan coinage.
13. *Corinth.* Æ. After 500 B.C. Later Corinthian coinage. Incuse anvil-mark replaced by type (head of Pallas), but with remains of incuse square still visible. Comp. Nos. 7 and 10.
14. *Corinth.* Æ. Later development of type of head of Pallas. Prototype of much of the later Italian coinage.
15. *Italy.* Campania. Æ. Derived from Corinthian coinage, and prototype of Roman coinage.

---

[37] It must be noted, as is said above in the beginning of the article, that it is impossible adequately to illustrate the evolution of types by the small number of coins figured. The pieces chosen are generally representative examples of a class of coins from which another class has sprung, and are rarely exact prototypes of any other type represented on the plate.

16. *Rome.* Æ. Early family denarius, the obverse derived from No. 15 (?).
17. *Macedon.* Philip II. (B.C. 359—336). AV. Introduction of a gold coinage into European Greece in place of the *daric* (No. 2), till then the medium of exchange.
18. *Gaul.* Gold. End of third century B.C. Imitation of Macedonian stater (No. 17).
19. *Britain.* Gold. Middle of second century B.C. Imitation of Gaulish coinage (No. 18), and in the second degree of the Macedonian (No. 17).
20. *Spain. Rhoda.* Silver. Drachm of the fourth century B.C.
21, 22. *Gaul.* Silver. Barbarous imitations of the coinage of Rhoda (No. 20) current in Gaul.
23. *Greece.* Silver. Tetradrachm of Alexander the Great. The inauguration of a new coinage of tetradrachms current throughout the Greek world, and designed to replace the older Athenian tetradrachms, whose standard they follow, and which were till then the general medium of exchange in silver, as the *darics* (No. 2) and after them the *philippi* (No. 17) were the media of exchange in gold.
24. *Syria.* Antiochus I. (Soter). Silver. Tetradrachm obviously modelled on the coinage of Alexander (No. 23), Heracles taking the place of Zeus.
25. *Syria.* Antiochus II. (Theos). Silver. Drachm of similar type. Apollo substituted for Heracles.
26. *Parthia.* Arsaces. Silver. Modelled on the coinage of Antiochus of Syria (No. 25).
27, 28. *Parthia.* Silver. Later Arsacid coinage, showing different developments of No. 26, the reverse type becoming more barbarous.
29. *Persia.* Silver. Sassanian. Earliest coinage. Ardeshir I. (A.D. 223—240). Copied from Arsacid coin No. 27.
30. *Persia.* Silver. Sassanian. Latest coinage. Khusrú II. (A.D. 591—628).
31. *Bokhara.* Silver. Barbarous imitation of Sassanian coinage current in Bokhara, seventh century A.D.
32. *Tabaristan.* Silver. Imitation of Sassanian coinage current in Tabaristan. Seventh century A.D.
33. *Syria.* Earliest Arab (Amawi) coinage struck at Damascus, A.H. 79 = A.D. 698, derived from the Sassanian (No. 30), perhaps through the coinage of Tabaristan (No. 32).
34. *Syria and Egypt.* Fatimite. Gold. Coin of El Mustansir (A.H. 427—495 = A.D. 1035—1094). Type of concentric circles, first modification in type of Arabic coins. It begins with El Mo'izz (A.D. 952—975).

35. *Anatolia.* Silver. Seljúkis, Kay Káwas I. (A.H. 607—616 = A.D. 1210—1219).
36. *Persia.* Silver. Hulágúis. Arghún (A.H. 683—690= A.D. 1284—1290).
37. *Persia.* Tímúr, with name of nominal sovereign Mahmúd. Struck at Samarkand, A.H. 795 = A.D. 1395.

These three are examples of the use of the square compartment within which part of the legend is inscribed. Nos. 35 and 36 belong to two opposite quarters of the Mohammedan world and show the likeness of the type. No. 37 is an example of the descent of the Hulágûí type to the dynasty of Tímúr.

38. *Turkey.* Sequin of Abd-el-Hamed I. (A.H. 1187—1203 = A.D. 1773—1789) struck at Constantinople, and bearing the *túghrá* or monogram of the Sultan.

We now return to another series of coins derived from the coinage of Alexander the Great.

39. *Bactria.* (Greek kings.) Silver. Euthydemus I. *circa* B.C. 220. Tetradrachm copied from tetradrachms of Seleucid kings of Syria (comp. No. 24).
40. *Susiana* (?) Barbarous copy of No. 39 or similar coin. These coins were also copied by the Kings of Characene, on the Persian Gulf.
41. *India.* Scythic kings. Azes. First century B.C. (?) Silver.
42. *India.* Scythic kings. Kadphises II. *Circa* Christian era. Gold.

These two are specimens of designs upon the coins of the Indo-Scythic kings which are evidently derived from the art of the earlier Greek kings of Bactria. 41 in its turn is probably the prototype.

43. *India.* Scythic king. Hooerkes. *Circa* A.D. 111—129. Gold.
44. *India.* Scythic king. Kanerkes. *Circa* A.D. 87—106. Gold.
45. *India.* A transition coin between the Indo-Scythic and the Gupta coinages. Gold.
46. *India.* Imitation of Indo-Scythic coinage under the influence of Sassanian coinage.
47. *India.* Earlier Gupta dynasty, miscalled Kanauj Guptas. Ghatotkacha. Gold. Compare obverses of Nos. 44, 45, 47 ; reverses of Nos. 44 and 47.
48. *India.* Earlier Gupta dynasty. Chandra Gupta II. Gold. The reverse has the figure of Lakshmi or Parvatí on lotus ; prototype of No. 50, reverse.

49. *India.* Sáh kings. Remotely derived from Greek Bactrian (coins of Menander). The reverse type (the *Chaitya*) is found on early Indian coins, and is perhaps derived from the fire-altar on the Sassanian coinage.
50. *India.* Later Gupta dynasty (of Saurásbtran). Obverse as obverse of last. Reverse from No. 48 (reverse).
51. *India* and *Bactria.* Scythic kings. Introduction of type of Bactrian bull.
52. *India.* Late reproduction of the same type. Silver.
53. *India.* Rajpút dynasty. Sri Syalapate Deva. Reproduction of Bactrian bull on Rajpút coinage. Silver.
54. *India.* Ghori. Mohammad ibn Sám. Copy of type from bull and horseman, type of Rajpút kings. Silver and copper mixed.
55. *India.* Ghori. Mohammad ibn Sám. Struck for Kanauj, and reproducing type of seated Lakshmi (see No. 48).

For Part II., Coins descended from the Roman coinage.

Nos. 56—91 represent classes derived from the coinage of Rome (the Roman Family).

56. *Roman.* Honorius, A.D. 395—423. Solidus. Reverse type, Victory. Gold.
57. *Roman Byzantine.* Mauricius Tiberius, A.D. 582—602. Triens. Reverse type, cross; extensively copied on Merovingian, &c., coins. Gold.
58. *Barbarian.* Odoacer. Siliqua. Earliest coin struck by barbarian king with portrait. Copied directly from Roman coinage. Silver.
59. *Merovingians.* Triens. Seventh century. Copied from coins of type of cross similar to reverse of No. 57. Gold.
60. *Merovingians.* Dorsted (Frisia). Seventh century. Ruder copy of coins of type of No. 57. Gold.
61. *Merovingians.* Paris. Reverse, curious type of cross ancrée. Gold.
62. *Lombards.* Cunipert, A.D. 688—700. Copied from type of No. 56. Gold.
63. *Roman.* Honorius. Triens. Gold.
64. *Suevians* in Lusitania (Portugal). Copied from No. 63. Gold.
65. *Roman.* Anastasius, or barbarian copy of. Gold.
66. *Visigoths* in Spain. Ruder copy of No. 65 or its prototype. Gold.
67. *Visigoths* in Spain. Leovigild, A.D. 573—586. Still ruder form of same type. Gold.

68. *Anglo-Saxons. Circa* 600 (?). Coin with Runic legend, derived from Merovingian coinage of type No. 59. Gold.
69. *Roman.* Magnus Maximus, A.D. 383—388. Solidus. Struck in London. Gold.
70. *Anglo-Saxon. Circa* 600 (?) Rude copy of No. 69.
71, 72. *Roman.* Constantine II. Copper denarii struck in London.
73. *Anglo-Saxon.* Sceatta. Type derived from Nos. 71 and 72. The obverse is copied from a coin of same obverse as No. 72, the reverse from No. 71 (reverse). Silver.
74. *Anglo-Saxon.* Has an obverse perhaps copied from a Merovingian coin. The reverse is copied from the Roman coins of type of 71.
75—78. *Anglo-Saxon.* Successive degradations of the same type, till a new type of a bird is produced on the obverse. (Comp. Evans, *British Coins,* Pl. XVI.) Silver.
79. *Carlovingian.* Pepin the Short (A.D. 752—768). The *new denarius* without any type. Silver.
80. *Carlovingian.* Charlemagne (A.D. 768—814). Ditto. Silver.
81. *Anglo-Saxon.* Northumbria. Styca. Likewise without type. Copper.
82—83. *Anglo-Saxon.* Offa, A.D. 757—796. Pennies. Introduction of the penny into England derived from the Carlovingian denarius. These are the types of Offa's pennies which most nearly follow types found on some Carlovingian denarii. For No. 82 compare Gariel, *Mon. Roy. de la Race Carlov.* Pl. VIII. Nos. 76—78 (rev.), 98 (rev.) ; for No. 83 comp. above fig. c1 (Merovingian), c2 (Carlovingian).
84—85. *Carlovingian.* Louis le Débonnaire (A.D. 814—840). Denarii. Temple type (two forms). Comp. above figs. e1, e2, e3, e4. Silver.
86. *Carlovingian.* Charles the Bald. Denarius. Type of Carolus monogram or Pitres type. See above p. 61. Silver.
87. *France.* Louis IX. (A.D. 1226—1270). Gros tournois. Tours type degraded from Temple type, with some influence of Pitres type. See p. 64, and figs. e1, e2, e3, e4. Silver.
88. *Germany.* Otho III., Emperor (A.D. 996—1002). German form of degradation of Temple type. Silver.
89. *England.* Æthelred II. (A.D. 978—1016). Penny. Silver.
90. *Danish Kings in Ireland.* Sihtric III. (A.D. 989—1029). Silver. Copied from No. 89.
91. *Denmark.* Harthacnut (A.D. 1035—1042). Silver.

Nos. 92—109 represent classes descended from the coinage of Rome through the Byzantine coinage.

92, 93. *Byzantine.* Constantine III. (A.D. 641—668). Solidi. Examples of characteristic Byzantine type of cross potent *haussée* upon three steps. Gold.

94. *Lombard Dukes of Beneventum.* Romvald II. (A.D. 707—733). Solidus. Gold. Copied directly from Byzantine coins of type of Nos. 92, 93.

95. *Papal.* Leo III. (795—816). Denarius. Silver. Showing influence of Byzantine coinage on obverse, and of Carlovingian on reverse. The earliest papal coins are those of Hadrian I., the immediate predecessor of Leo III., (Floravantes, *Pont. Roma. Denarii*, p. 1), and these are of the same type as the coins of the Dukes of Beneventum, No. 94.

96. *Byzantine.* Leo VI. and Constantine X. (*circ.* A.D. 910). Solidus Byzantinus, or *besant.* Gold.

97. *Byzantine.* Romanus III. (A.D. 1027—1034). Solidus Byzantinus, or *besant.* Gold.

98. *Venice.* Enrico Dandolo (A.D. 1192—1205). Ducato d'argento. This is the first departure from the German Imperial type on coins of Venice. It is evidently derived from the Byzantine coinage. Both Nos. 96 and 97 may have served as prototypes for this type. On the left shoulder of the Virgin crowning the Emperor are four pellets, which are reproduced on the shoulder of St. Mark holding standard (No. 98).

99. *Venice.* Aloysio Mocenigo II. (A.D. 1700—1709). Sequin. This gives the unchanged type of the sequin from the time of its introduction by Giovanni Dandolo (A.D. 1279—1289). The piece chosen is the immediate prototype of the one which follows.

100. *North Africa.* Barbarous imitation in brass of No. 99, in which the type and even the letters of the legend are faintly traceable. Thus the MOCEN. of 99 is reproduced in the NOCEN of 100.

101. *Servia.* Stephan III. Orosius (A.D. 1240—1272). Copied from the Byzantine type No. 96. Silver.

102. *Milan.* First Republic, A.D. 1250—1312. Silver. The type of this coin is derived remotely from the seated figure of Christ in the Byzantine coinage (comp. Nos. 96, 97). The gold coinage of the same period, which for want of a specimen in the National Collection cannot be reproduced here, is more directly and obviously derived from the Byzantine gold coinage. (See Gnecchi, *Monete di Milano*, Tav. IV. No. 1.)

The type of this coin may be taken as a general example of the type of the front-face seated figure common on the coinage of the greater part of Europe from the twelfth to the fourteenth centuries and later, and derived originally from the Byzantine type of the seated figure of Christ.

103. *Byzantine.* Constantine XII. (A.D. 1042—1055). Silver. Half figure of Virgin.

104. *Aquileia.* Patriarch. Bertoldo, Duke of Meran (A.D. 1218—1225). Silver type, taken from type of No. 103.

105. *Germany.* Eleventh century. Silver. Both obverse and reverse show a certain influence of the Byzantine coinage (see p. 79). The coin actually chosen is of Ecbert, Duke of Misnia (A.D. 1088—1090). But others of the same type (no well preserved specimen is in the British Museum) were struck by the contemporary German emperors.

106—107. *Denmark.* Magnus the Good (A.D. 1042—1047), and Svend Estrithsen (A.D. 1047—1076). Silver. The obverse types of these pieces are obviously copied from Byzantine types (comp. Nos. 96, 97). The reverses are of the English type of No. 91.

108. *Florence.* Silver florin. First coined 1181. This type is probably remotely derived from the type of the half-figure of Christ on the Byzantine coinage. (Comp. Sabatier, *Mon. Byz.*, Pl. XLVI. *seqq.*)

109. *Florence.* Gold florin. First coined in 1252. Derived from silver florin (No. 108).

With the introduction of this coin (the *fiorino d'oro*) a new era begins in the coinage of Western Europe, and this era lies outside the limits of the present enquiry. It is for this reason that the gold florin stands last in the series.

REPRINTED FROM THE NUMISMATIC CHRONICLE,

Vol. V., Third Series, Pages 165—198,
Vol. VI., Pages 41—95.

LONDON:

1886.

PLATES

MORPHOLOGY.

Plate I.

MORPHOLOGY.

Plate II.

MORPHOLOGY.

Plate III.

MORPHOLOGY.

PLATE IV.

79 80 81 82 83 84 85 86 87 88 89 90 91 92 93 94 95

MORPHOLOGY.

PLATE V.

MORPHOLOGY.

PLATE VI.